REDFIN DIARIES

A life in the year of a roach enthusiast

MARK EVERARD

Coch-y-Bonddu Books
2013

REDFIN DIARIES
A life in the year of a roach enthusiast

Written and illustrated by Mark Everard

First published by Coch-y-Bonddu Books Ltd, Machynlleth, 2013

ISBN 978 1 904784 60 9

Coch-y-Bonddu Books Ltd, Machynlleth, Powys, SY20 8DG
01654 702837
www.anglebooks.com

Contents

SPRING:

This book is dedicated to all those who love roach and the aquatic life of which they are an intimate part, and particularly to those who work tirelessly to protect or improve the waters in which roach swim.

The young author, sometime around 1970, already
displaying acute symptoms of the 'roach bug'

A fine Bristol Avon brace of 2 lb 9 oz and 2 lb 8 oz roach, October 2007

Foreword by Keith Berry

IN MARCH 2006, I had the good fortune to hook and land a huge roach from a Northern Irish lough. That fish weighed an unbelievable 4 lb 4 oz, one ounce over the existing record. After verification that its capture fulfilled all the criteria in place at the time it was duly accepted as the new British record roach by the British Record (Rod Caught) Fish Committee. The lough that was home to the roach was rarely fished and its potential was completely unknown. On a pike fishing trip with my son the previous winter, I had observed what looked to me like rolling roach, but these fish seemed too big to be roach. The sight of those fish stayed with me for the weeks and months after that fateful session. In March of that year, I decided it was time to tackle the fish I had seen using traditional swingtip and maggot feeder tactics taught to me by my father. I was on the water with a fishing buddy. The scene was set: it was the usual wet Irish day, starting off damp and getting wetter as the day went on. The morning was pretty uneventful other than the odd rolling fish and an occasional twitch on the swingtip. In the late afternoon, as I refilled my feeder, a large fish rolled close in off the baited area. My tenching head took over and I dropped the feeder on top of the fish. Within minutes, the swingtip straightened out and I was into a fish that was to change my life. The roach was to be the first of three over 4 lb (though one was a recapture of the record fish), and no fewer than thirteen others over 3 lb 6 oz.

Around the time the roach was accepted as the new record, I received a phone call at work from some guy who introduced himself with, 'You won't know me but my name is Mark Everard'. I had never met Mark but had seen his photos in the angling press and was aware of his exploits with roach. He congratulated me on my capture and went on to explain that he was just putting the finishing touches to his latest book (*The Complete Book of the Roach*) and would be delighted if I were to permit him to include a photo and an account of my capture, if this could be done in time before the book went to print. If I were to be honest, I thought the man to be a little eccentric! But I warmed to his manner and his enthusiasm was infectious. How could I say no? I found out later that Mark had known about the capture of my big fish ever since I had first reported it as, being an eminent aquatic scientist, the photographs of the fish had been sent to him to be identified. Mark had not contacted me until all the paperwork had been completed for fear of compromising my record claim.

Over the next week or two, Mark phoned me a number of times to discuss my inclusion in his book and, as my roach captures continued, I found myself contacting Mark to share my excitement. We talked about roach in particular and angling in general. A good friendship was beginning to form, we started to talk about everyday things like families and work. But, unlike some other enquirers, Mark never once asked me for information on the roach water. Around a year after first encountering Mark, we had become firm friends and I decided I would invite him over to fish the lough for himself. I can still recall during that phone call listening to Mark like an excited boy announcing to his wife, Jake, that, 'Keith has invited me over to his special lake!' I picked Mark up at a wet and windy Belfast City airport. We embraced as if we had known each other for a lifetime, though in reality we were in each other's company for the first time. I had been very nervous about the trip. How would this rough Belfast housing estate guy deal with four nights in the close company of a well-educated prominent scientist? Mark had travelled for a couple of days of craic and I think deep down inside he just wanted to be on the water that was home to so many massive roach. I, on the other hand, had other ideas: my mission was to help Mark beat his personal best roach. Mark is a traditional river angler and I recall him clearing the supermarket shelf of its bread, planning to take the water apart on his terms. I shoved a box of maggots in his direction and suggested that when he got fed up blanking on bread he should give those a try. Mark's success came quickly, on the first night in fact. But that story is told within these pages so I won't spoil it for you, only to recall Mark standing ankle deep in the ice fringed margins in the dead of night wearing nothing on his feet but stripy multi-coloured socks, staring into his landing net muttering words unbefitting of a man of his standing. But that is what fishing can do to you and this confirmed my earlier suspicions, totally eccentric!

Mark returned to fish the lough with me a number of times but we could not better the results of that first trip. The water became harder and harder and sightings of rolling fish became fewer and further between. The fish that I caught were estimated to be around twelve years old, around the upper age limit for roach and there did not seem to be a similar stamp of roach coming behind. It was sad, but nothing lasts forever. However, one positive was that those times fishing together helped to cement a very solid friendship. I did visit England most years in pursuit of tench, and Mark always made a point of visiting me bearing gifts of beer and hot takeaway food. It is often quoted that angling is a great leveller and I like to think that the friendship that Mark and I share is definitive proof that people from two different worlds can become so close because of their enjoyment of fishing.

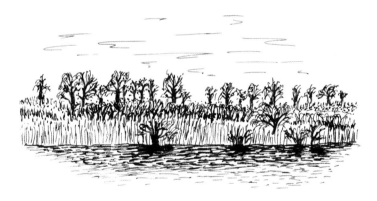

The rest of the book demonstrates how Mark has always applied his scientific mind to pursuing roach in every environment from large rivers to small ponds, from the heat of summer to biting frosty days. Remarkably, he has been doing this, constantly innovating and experimenting as well as writing about and reporting big roach and other species to the angling press, since the 1970s. But always he does so with humour and a huge amount of respect for his quarry, and a near reverence for big roach in particular. In *Redfin Diaries*, which is structured around the turn of the seasons, he shares glimpses into notable moments and shares not a few useful tips learnt over his long angling career. *A life in the year of a roach enthusiast* indeed!

Mark always tells me he thinks I'm a great roach angler, but I tell him I'm just a good tench angler who occasionally catches decent roach! But being offered that compliment from someone like Mark, who as I write has had 11 roach of 3 lb or more from different rivers and from my lough, and well over 900 roach of 2 lb or more, is something of which I am extremely proud.

This is a book for the enthusiast but also the countryman, for the specimen hunter but also the romantic. I hope you enjoy it as much as I have, and will return to it often for pleasure and also to pick up some useful tips.

Keith Berry, holding the British rod-caught record roach of 4 lb 4 oz

Casting off

ROACH. WHERE DOES ONE START in the telling of tales of roach great and small, the many ways and means of catching them, and the often-beautiful places in which they live?

There is no obvious starting point, as both roach and roach fishing adapt with the changing seasons. Far more though seems to have been written about the capture of sizeable roach during the 'sweet spot' at the back end of the river season, when they are reaching their peak pre-spawning condition and size and are feeding in earnest in winter flows, than at any other time. My intention is, however, to tell you of roach (and big roach in particular) that have swum my way the whole year round. Roach that I have encountered throughout more than fifty years of dabbling at the water's edge, forty of them as a committed (some may prefer the term 'certifiable') and tolerably successful specimen roach fisher. Some of these roach are recent and huge, others are big and less contemporary. All are treasured.

The first roach I was to meet was neither recent nor big. That first encounter was in the sunnier shallow waters of a childhood of distinctly dappled shade, specifically in the late spring of 1960 when I was only two. It is then that I had made the progression from sticklebacks caught on cane and cotton to using a real rod in a real river, Kent's River Medway. The memory is vivid and clear still, indeed far more so than most of later childhood. Most of my memories from those fledgling days are suffused with the sounds, smells and sights of long days next to fresh waters of one type or another.

My first day with a real rod on the river was special. The rod itself was not. It was a hand-me-down from an uncle, a heavy beast of whole cane with a herringbone pattern branded into it that had not been used since before the Second World War. It took all of my strength just to lift it to raise the gaudy float into and out of the water. The rod was coupled with a centrepin reel of similar vintage and decrepitude.

This was well before the time when centrepins were considered to be 'classic', and this particular one was never going to gain that accolade. 'Old and worn out' was a fairer description, but this was nevertheless 'grown up' tackle, and I was certainly not complaining.

My float was of the same era, a bulbous cork body on a cane stem, the upper part painted a lurid red. The float sat prominently in the water riding the gentle current, in fact probably buoyant enough to ride out a tsunami. But it was mine, and served well to suspend a blob of bread paste down in the dark waters beneath a screed of cut grass that had blown in from a freshly-cut playing field.

I sat there on the bank top in the spring sunshine for a long while, staring down at the gaudy float tip. Then something must have distracted me (which to be honest is hardly surprising if you have ever fished with young kids), and when I looked back the float had ducked out of sight beneath the floating blades of grass.

I lifted the heavy rod as best I could, raising my 'marker buoy' float out of the water and with it a pulsating sliver of silver. I was paralysed in amazement, gazing spellbound at the helpless fish as it flickered this way and that. I also had no idea what to do about it, so I jumped about and shouted with excitement.

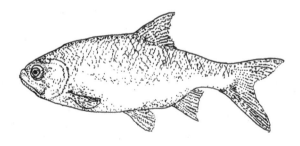

As fate would have it, my father had just gone to a kiosk close by to buy an ice cream. On hearing my screams, he had naturally assumed that I had fallen in. In no time, he bounded across to where I sat, ice creams dropped in panic. I recall him being there to unhook the fish and share my moment of rapturous excitement. Looking back with the older eyes of a parent, I can only assume that his experience was rather less one of unbounded joy and more one of getting over a horrible shock!

He held the roach up close to me to, showing me its red fins and eye and also how to unhook it, and then allowed me to hold it up close for inspection in wetted hands before slipping it back into its mysterious world.

This was one of my warmest childhood memories, as sadly our lives, mine and my father's, were to coincide for a cruelly short time. Whether this memory is cause or merely catalyst I cannot say, but I do know that roach (and other fishes of many types) have swum deep in my life ever since.

And yes, I have had my share of truly great fish in the 'back end' of the river season. But some terrific roach have come my way throughout all the seasons of the year and of my life, and to a variety of different methods.

It is these that I want to share with you through these pages, in part for your enjoyment but there may just also be some things to learn from the occasional rewards of my life-long passion and its unending experimentation.

SUMMER

SUMMER DAZE

1

Yellow water lily flowers about to burst open under warm June sunshine

Summer Daze

WHEN THE SUN beats down and flows recede and aquatic plants grow lush as currents decline, the quest for sizeable roach may not be the most obvious of pursuits.

With the fish on the mend from spawning and (even when recovered) well below the peak weight they will attain when packing on roe during the winter, many anglers turn their attentions to other quarry. Indeed, for me, summer is most often now a time for family and fun, research and other work commitments deferred from the end of the river season, and for fish spotting. Any remaining time is then generally turned to tench, barbel, dace and other classically 'summer species'.

However, roach, including big roach, are most assuredly there for the catching. They are highly unlikely to be where you found them in the back end of the river season, and will almost certainly be behaving and feeding quite differently from then, but make no mistake they are there for the taking.

In fact, with the hindsight distilled from writing these few summer chapters, I wonder why I have neglected them for so long.

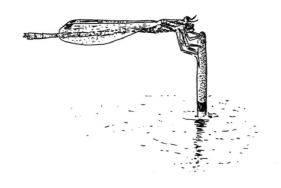

Fine roach to a shade over 2 lb were the periodic reward of free-lining
bread flake in an estate lake during the baking summer of 1976

2 lb+ roach safely within the folds of my landing net by a summer river

The Old Estate Lake

TO BE PERFECTLY honest, life circumstances meant that my school days, those supposedly 'happiest times of your life' were largely unremitting misery. Even after all this time, most recollections are still simply locked away. Some burst through in a kind of faded monochrome, and are as rapidly rationalised then set aside. However, a precious few blossom with the vivid hues of the summer days on which they were imprinted. And many of these circulate around an old, largely forgotten estate lake nestled in a bowl of woodland and pasture.

Like many of these types of waters, the lake was formed in order to provide a water supply by damning a stream valley, probably in this case some time at the end of the nineteenth century. Also like many, it had silted up considerably in the intervening century. Yet, when the summer sun turned its shallow waters tepid and the yellow water lilies spread their broad leaves and thrust their vivid yellow flowers upwards to greet the azure sky, the rich fish fauna came out to bask.

Many were the invariably solitary but always contented pre-dawn sessions that I enjoyed casting my float out to lily fringes in the half light, offering bread, worm or, on such rare occasions as I could scrape together the (pre-decimal) pennies, maggots to what lay beneath. I'd marvel at the bursts of bubbles as fish mouthed the sediment in the dark depths below, sitting taut with anticipation as I willed my float to dance or dip. My first ever tench came from that silent estate lake, running just as much like a train as Mr Crabtree had promised. And feeling curiously velvet to the touch and emanating that evocative fruity mustiness.

Many more tench came my way, either from the lily fringe by half-light or from the dappled shade by day as I crouched expectantly over free-lined offerings flicked out under the broad, full-leafed boughs of the mature oaks that fringed much of the water. Rudd too (and some thumping big ones at that), mainly interspersing the crepuscular tench action by the lily fringe.

And roach as well, including big ones. As I look back forty years later, I only realise now the quality of local sport that I had stumbled across, and the respite that the tranquil lake offered me from the noise and mess of life beyond its oaken embrace. The roach there occasionally fell to my float-fished dawn offerings, but I had my own special and highly effective way of picking out the largest amongst them at a time when all other folks considered them uncatchable. When the sun had climbed to its zenith, burning down at its hottest, when only mad dogs and this particular young Englishman ventured forth with rod in hand, those were the magical times to conjure up big roach from that old estate lake.

There was a saying about fish in the late 1960s and into the 1970s that, '...if you can see them then you can't catch them'. Many were the anglers who proved this true for themselves by finding that the only reaction their legered or float-fished offerings got was, at best, indifference or, more frequently, blind panic.

For me though, it was clear that although these basking fish were lying close to the surface film, and were therefore extraordinarily sensitive to disturbances even as slight as the shadow of a passing blackbird, they were also hungry. That, by basking in the warmest water, their appetites had been inevitably stimulated by the boost this gives to the digestive system of a cold-blooded beast.

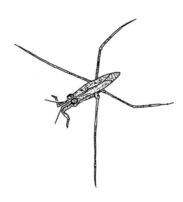

The rig that I settled on to address this challenge was simplicity itself. My only functional rod was a general-purpose, 12ft glass-fibre float rod and my reel a small Mitchell fixed spool. This I loaded with gossamer 2 lb test line, greased with Vaseline to make it float in the surface film, tying a size 12 hook to the end. Bait was a simple disc torn from a sliced white loaf, delicately hooked to retain its fluffy texture then dipped in the water's edge momentarily before casting to increase its weight and range. I could cast that bait accurately to thirty yards where it would plop softly, coming to rest just beneath the surface film courtesy of the bubbles trapped within its fluffy texture. As basking fish encountered this soft, tasty offering, it required the least of efforts to slurp it in. Then, all hell would break loose in the shallow waters as I tightened up on seeing the bait vanish, or else watching the trailing line describe a 'V' across the dusty surface. Or, if the fish were cruising more actively, I'd wait for one to sip in something from the surface film, noting that a comfortable cruising speed for the fish was at or slightly slower than the rate at which ripples propagated across the languid lake surface. Flicking out a fragment of weighted flake in front of that ripple frequently resulted in the feeding fish engulfing my tasty offering instantly.

Long days with exams over and no other pressures. Happy days of wet shoes and moist nets. Productive days that I look back on now with fondness, but also with not a little awe at the sheer abundance and quality of the fish on offer. It was, with hindsight, one of those serendipitous chances of lucking in to the right place at the right time, with a flexible mind and with time to enjoy it. Above all, I was in the 'Goldilocks zone' when a couple of strong year classes of fish in perfect circumstances resulted in specimen roach proliferating and offering the potential for the most exquisite of sport. I have enjoyed similar luck sometimes over many subsequent years, on the Hampshire Avon, the Bristol Avon and on a couple of stillwaters. I have the hindsight now to know that these circumstances never last. And that, in that far off scorching summer, life was kind to a fledgling specimen angler by setting a compass for the long road ahead.

Curiously, no one else seemed able or minded to break free of accepted methods to sample this red-finned bounty, and the hidden lake was usually mine alone to enjoy. These then were days of quiet solitude. Shared only with the sinuous grass snakes that swam the sun-warmed waters, the swallows that skimmed to drink and the ghosts of mist that danced up from the calm lake surface as the sun first peaked through the lake's fringing oak guardians at the first kiss of dawn. These were solitary days that were never dull, lonely or too long. They captivated attention and anticipation and were never anything but over-brimming with life.

I had my first 2 lb roach one burning summer day when, by common consensus, no roach should have been stirring. Then in successive summers, a couple more big ones amongst many, many chunky fish deceived while warming their backs in the summer sun. It only ended when I went up to university in London and a smorgasbord of life's other pleasures and priorities took over, at least for a while.

I have never been back to that musty old estate lake. It is wise advice never to return, for things can be different but never the same. But those sunny days of roach 'from the top' live on, and have left their indelible mark on me in terms of my deep love of quiet waters, and the valuable lesson of remaining flexible when approaching supposedly uncatchable roach as indeed any other species of fish.

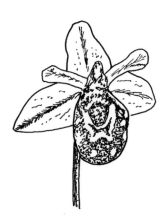

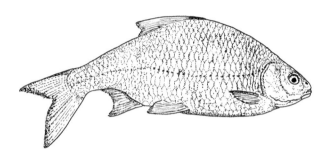

A fine 2 lb 11 oz roach taken whilst roving a near-static reach of summer river
in the early 1990s

Life and Death in the Lily Pads

I DON'T USE fish as live bait. I just don't like it. I know that I have gone to some lengths in my book, *The Complete Book of the Roach*, about how the nervous system and brain structure of fish doesn't result in them feeling pain in the sense that we know it. But I know too that they can nonetheless become distressed and this, in a sentient vertebrate like a fish, is something with which I am simply not comfortable.

For many years during the 1980s my unease with using living baits even extended to maggots and worms. It is a little bit difficult in practice to say exactly where cruelty begins and ends. Does a lack of legs, in the case of such apparently dumb invertebrates as maggots and worms, mean that they are fair game to be used as living bait? Taking the analogy a little further, is using a fresh green pea (and believe me they do catch fish) cruel given that it too is a living, albeit vegetative being?

The matter of what is sentient, what is alive or not, and what can suffer pain and what is cruelty, is a huge topic covered by many world religions. We're certainly not going to crack it in this book on roach angling! But, as pragmatic anglers, rather than as Buddhist monks committed to the taking of no life, we have to find our own personal moral place with these issues of life and death.

There are some baits that I've used overseas which have left me feeling more than a little uneasy, but they're generally accepted in the places I have used them. For example, live crickets are a staggeringly successful bait for yellowfish and other quarry in South Africa, not to mention extremely effective for black bass and many other species in the Americas.

All this musing about life and death of course brings me to caddis larvae. I know how devastatingly effective caddis larvae, removed from their cases, can be for roach, dace and a good deal of other species besides. Indeed, they were once a staple bait that could be purchased from tackle dealers. But the reservations I hold about their use revolve largely around my own soft-heartedness, I am rather fond of these cute little larvae and feel uncomfortable impaling them on a hook. However, devastatingly effective they can be as bait.

The first time I witnessed their efficacy at first hand was in that summer lake where I learnt the power of free-lining bread for sunbathing roach. There was one other lad who used to fish the lake on a very occasional basis, and his method was to fish caddis larvae under a light waggler float just beneath the water's surface. Whilst he never caught anywhere near as many of those sumptuous roach as I did, I certainly saw him bank a respectable number of fish on caddis larvae sipped from close to the water's surface.

In the tepid and static waters of many summer rivers with their flows stilled by seasonal drought exacerbated by excessive abstraction, roach can often be seen using the shelter of lily stems and the undersides of lily leaves. And, if you sit and gaze carefully enough you may see them grazing these underwater surfaces for tasty morsels.

As a biologist, I can tell you with some certainty that snails and other molluscs are a staple part of the diet of summer roach. However, as an experimental angler, I can also tell you that I've tried to present all manner of snails on the hook over the years with almost no success. I'm not the only one that has tried and failed either! Quite why a snail on the hook ceases to be as appealing remains a perpetual mystery.

What is certain though is that a caddis larva presented immediately against these same submerged surfaces will often be seized voraciously. It is at this time of year that a roach pole can be used to the most devastating effect, the overhead cover of lily pads shielding the pole tip from the roach beneath whilst the bait is presented on gossamer tackle under a light float or else fished by sight on a free line. A caddis larva presented thus, once cruising roach have been located and patiently stalked, is an immensely attractive and effective bait. But the fact remains that I am still uneasy about using these charismatic insects.

The good news is that very fine particles of bread can serve almost as well when presented in the form of tiny fragments of bread flake or else as punched bread on fine-wired hooks. Maggots too have their place. I have certainly taken a good number of 2 lb roach on the former and a few on the latter when rivers are in their lethargic summer condition.

But the opportunities do not stop here. Take an aquarium net with you to the water's edge, swish it around in the marginal vegetation, and you will find an array of organisms which the roach will also be rooting around for. Water shrimps are absolutely devastating. Water slaters (which closely resemble woodlice) are also tasty morsels for a roach. But a word of caution about assuming that land-based woodlice will also be as enticing: it seems that there is some bitter or otherwise distasteful chemical secreted by woodlice that positively repels roach and other fish, and I say this from having tried them many times on the hook with uniformly disappointing outcomes. But always remember that, if you can find a tasty looking morsel in the riverside vegetation, so can the roach. Dragonfly larvae, for example, are highly sought-after, though I have the same queasiness about using them despite having also seen their proven effectiveness for yellowfish when fishing in South Africa.

Silkweed may be an old-fashioned bait but it is one that has its place from time to time, and in particular circumstances. However, the main problem in the modern era is that our rivers are so enriched by nutrient substances from agriculture and other forms of effluent that there is a great proliferation of filamentous algae of types that are not particularly palatable to roach. Also, a little fragment of soft weed presented where more wiry species of algae abound is unlikely to be either noticed or consumed.

However, it is surprising just what baits hungry roach will be happy to pick up when grazing these submerged vegetation surfaces. I've had them on sweetcorn, stewed wheat, tares, small redworms, and even on a pellet though I'm not a great fan of them. Just about the only consistent lesson I have learnt about the use of baits for summer roach grazing submerged surfaces is to avoid using loose feed. Loose feed is a certain recipe for disaster, mainly because it tends to draw in hoards of minnows which will then worry your hook bait to pieces! Also, uneaten bait will tend to fall to the riverbed and the roach may well follow it downwards and out of sight. (This need not be a disaster if you intend to fish for them with the 'lift method', particularly into dusk, as I describe elsewhere in this book.)

Although it is generally accepted that the pole is best fished from a static box, on which the angler is seated to work the swim and draw in fish, I take a diametrically opposite approach. For me, the pole is superb for mobile fishing and I'm happy to work miles of riverbank lugging my pole, landing net, and a small bag of bait and accessories. Stalking in this manner, picking out roach here and there by sight or from likely-looking holes in weeds or, when the current picks up, runs between stands of submerged vegetation, can be a fruitful approach. It is not an ideal method for fishing public waters though, as dog-walkers and children are invariably attracted by the weird sight of someone carrying a huge long shaft of carbon and will demand to know what it is all about!

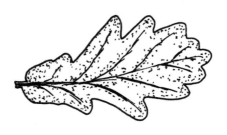

But if you take yourself to a quiet stretch of water with some flow and habitat diversity, a good day is often to be enjoyed. Indeed, I remember one particularly excellent day under the summer sun when I had the good fortune to present a tiny flake of bread and winkle out a beautiful roach of 2 lb 5 oz, all gilded flanks with fins made vivid red by the pigments that the fish had absorbed from months of feeding on insects. It was not the biggest summer roach that I've ever had, and by some degree, but it may have been the most uniquely beautiful. And then, maybe a half-hour later, in a run of slightly more streamy water between ribbon-weed patches, a dace of exactly a pound came to the same offering. A 'magic double', as the late and great Richard Walker had coined the capture of a roach of two pounds or more and a dace of a pound or over from the same sitting. Not my biggest magic double either, but certainly the least expected under a burning summer sky with both fish in their most devastatingly beautiful summer livery.

There is a time and a place for this non-traditional approach, as indeed there is for every method. But do recognise that, even in the most tempting swim, the use of this method under power lines is a seriously bad idea! Not only is there a much higher chance of you actually touching the power lines with an extremely long and highly conductive shaft of carbon fibre, but there is also a far greater risk of electricity arcing down to earth through it. If you don't understand these risks, do find out, as the threat to life and limb is very real. Never, ever take a chance. Otherwise, all of our early preoccupations about life and death amongst the lily pads may have a far more macabre and personal meaning!

A fine brace of early November roach of 2 lb 7 oz and 2 lb 6 oz,
trotted from the Bristol Avon in 2008

Hemped out on the Stour

THE ALLURE OF hemp, particularly for roach in summer rivers, is legendary.

Hemp is the seed of a variety of the cannabis plant. In the past, this has given it a bad reputation due to a misplaced belief of it acting as a drug. This misconception in turn led to bans on its use in a number of fisheries during the 1960s, and some of these bans remain in force even today. Certainly, hemp does seem to have a powerful capacity to attract and preoccupy fish of many species, particularly roach and barbel. However, scientific analysis does not bear out that this effect is in any way connected with THC (tetrahydrocannibol), the active ingredient of marijuana. In fact, virtually all strains of hemp have no, or at least minimal, traces of THC in their makeup.

But, as many of us know from personal experience, hemp can drive roach and many other species of fish into a feeding frenzy. This effect is both visual and chemical.

The visual attractiveness of hemp is obviously maximised in clear-water conditions. Loose-fed hemp, half-a-dozen grains per cast to encourage fish to rise up in the water column seeking more, can drive a roach shoal into a feeding frenzy at pretty much any time of the year when the water is clear, and particularly in warmer conditions. I've seen it happen many times and my belief is that the falling hemp grains closely resemble certain types of small, dark water snail that thrive on summer vegetation, part of the defensive behaviour of which is to detach themselves from plants and to fall through the water column away from would-be predators. Roach, dace and other river fish are well attuned to intercepting these falling black snails in flowing waters.

And, of course, there is something particularly pleasant about the smell of stewed or grilled hemp. Just a few grains falling into gravel on the riverbed can drive barbel, dace and roach wild, as they rip up the riverbed to root out the source of the attractive aroma.

Put together, this chemical and visual attraction can make hemp an amazingly effective bait in the right circumstances.

One of the most frenetic afternoon's sport that have I ever enjoyed, thanks to the hemp, was on a sunny summer's day in the clear waters of the Dorset Stour. I am not going to tell you exactly where. However, I'm sure that you can work out the approximate location when I tell you about a not-so-productive day on the same water. Venturing there one fine day for a quiet afternoon's sport, a Vulcan bomber suddenly loomed out of nowhere, immediately above my head, and banked with its afterburners full on. The ground shook. I shook. The trees shook. And I'm sure that, if the roach had fillings in their pharyngeal teeth, they would have shaken too. The Vulcan was, in turn, soon followed by a couple of Harriers on a low-level strafing run, then the whole Red Arrows team in full display mode, and then a gigantic Russian jet freighter and a whole cavalcade of other military aviation which, unbeknown to me, were part of a major air show a very short way from my chosen tranquil spot by the river!

That day, not even hemp could switch the fish on in quite the way I'd hoped. However, this was a stretch of the Stour that I liked very much, and on which the hemp seemed to work remarkably well. I was to be seen there pursuing roach quite frequently when the sun shone during those now-distant summer months.

But getting back to the frenetic day's sport, it all started when, standing in waders in the river margin, I found a decent shoal of roach and started to feed them patiently, half-a-dozen or so grains every minute. Soon the numbers of fish increased until I had built up a substantial, excited shoal right in front of me, competing with each other for every grain. The average size of these fish was pretty good too, including many big fish with some specimens of up to an estimated 2½lb. As I continued to feed the shoal, I inevitably dropped a grain or two here or there. Some of these great big roach were literally darting in between my waders to beat their smaller shoal-mates to them to intercept the stray hemp grains. When you spend as many years as I have stalking fish, and know how wary a big roach can be, this boldness was nothing short of revelatory.

So, worked up nicely, it was time to get amongst these fish and see which wanted to come out and join me on the bank. Often, I will cook up a few tares, offering one of these small brown peas on the hook as the roach tend to prefer them due to their slightly larger size. At other times, I will sink the hook into the pit of a hemp grain leaving the point exposed where the seed has split on cooking. But today I was trying something new.

This was back in the late 1980s, and so you have to understand that when one of my good friends handed me a brown envelope containing a mystery gift I was hesitant to find it contained a perfect, hand-crafted replica of a well-boiled hemp grain complete with an acrylic 'root' poking out the bottom. This friend had a well-developed sense of humour, so my natural instinct was that I was being 'wound up' once again. Perhaps this seems naïve today, in an age when one can buy plastic versions of pretty much every natural or synthetic bait, and of proven efficacy, but that could not be said at the time. On that long-gone summer day, I was going to try out my new piece of synthetic hemp for the first time on the unsuspecting fish of the Dorset Stour.

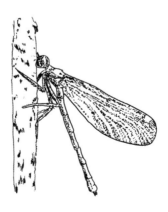

I rigged up a soft twelve-foot rod and closed-faced reel with the lightest waggler float in my box, shot bulked by the float base so that they would not be inadvertently mistaken for and intercepted as falling hemp grains from which many false bites would ensue. Then, taking a leap into the unknown, I tied a size 14 hook to the end of my line and nicked this through the soft rubber part of the synthetic hemp grain. All the while, I had maintained constant feeding to keep the fish hunting and competing to the point that the water positively boiled when I merely swung my empty hand as if throwing in more bait. So much for stalking and remaining invisible!

The following hour was a serious eye-opener. I cast in the light waggler and, instantly, the plastic grain was engulfed by a chunky roach of about 1½ lbs which fought bravely in the warm water. When they are competing really actively, the bulkier fish can often be the first to hit the hook bait as they barge their smaller peers out of the way. Not a bad start. Between casts, I kept the free offerings going in to maintain the confidence of the fish, lobbing my bait into the water after a few free cycles of offerings. On every cast, the plastic grain was engulfed almost immediately, always before it had time to sink more than a couple of inches below the warm surface of the river.

Fish after fish, driven crazy for my bait, succumbed to the resistance of the light float rod and was summarily drawn quickly downstream to get it out of the shoal.

As the sun dipped and the shoal thinned, I had caught comfortably in excess of 40 lbs (and probably even more), of plump Stour roach of all sizes. I had put none in a keepnet, and paused only to weight the biggest. Amazingly, these included nine fish between 1 lb 15 oz and 1 lb 15 oz 12dr! Not a two-pounder amongst them. Should I be disappointed? No. It was a fabulous day's fishing by any standards, leaving me a legacy of rich and enduring memories and a whole bunch of lessons.

I would like to say that I treasure that beautifully-crafted plastic grain still, but the truth is that it got snagged on a submerged weed bed on my last cast and, as the fine line parted with a 'ping', that was the last I saw of it.

I became a firm believer in the power of hemp, and a confident proponent of artificial hemp on the hook. Now, of course, one can go to any tackle shop to buy authentic plastic replicas of hemp and many other types of bait besides. But, in the intervening years, I had to make do with crafting my own plastic hemp using little black plastic beads cut in half then stuck together with a small blob of acrylic sealant, or else using a small pellet cut from a Liquorice Allsort with a bread punch. Life is somewhat easier today!

Above all, I learned what an enjoyable way hemping is to take roach from summer rivers, including sizeable roach. Hemp is such clean bait too, and you can travel as light as you like. Furthermore, when the fish are in the mood, they can be absolutely crazy for it.

A male roach (the top fish with spawning tubercles still visible) cruises
with a chub in the sun-warmed upper layer of the Bristol Avon

Rock 'n Roll on a Summer Stream

THE 1970S WEREN'T all about sex and drugs and rock 'n roll you know, or at least not for me. (Okay if I am to be totally honest, most of the second half of the 1970s was.) But rock 'n roll was the only part of that unholy trinity that I really got into during the first half of the decade, the long, hot summers of which were spent rather more in stalking the rivers of Sussex than in chasing other highs.

I've already written of my penchant for fishing by sight in that era using free-lined baits: bread, worms or other bank-side finds with some dead-baits thrown in during the winter. No river that was within strike range of my battered old bike (bought for two quid from another boy desperate for cigarette money) was safe from me.

I spent long days watching and casting, stalking or lying back in lush bank-top vegetation, during which I rarely encountered another human being until encroaching dusk drove me away. My bike had no lights you see, and the price of batteries would anyhow have been beyond my straightened means. And there were more important things to buy, like a few hooks and a small loaf, the modest price of which bought freedom and paradise unbridled, all mine to enjoy.

I learned so much during those now-distant days by watching and experimenting, seeing what worked and what didn't, and what I did that scared the fish or concealed me from them. I found, for example, that the ultimate camouflage was not to be found in army surplus stores but by the simple expedient of removing my shirt.

I suppose that common sense should lead us to realise that nearly four billion years of evolution would equip us with some features of natural camouflage, but it was a revelation nonetheless. Thus unadorned from the waist up, I'd stalk tiny and neglected streams right up behind trout, making use of their blind spots, to flick out worms that would likely to be engulfed hungrily. Chub and dace too, and rudd, in the stiller reaches.

Those hot summer days often found me chasing chub in various reed and lily-fringed channels. I think that this was for three primary reasons: they were often the most clearly visible of fishes cruising the warm subsurface; they had big mouths and unfailingly hungry stomachs; and, of course, they were often the biggest species present (aside from pike which are another story altogether).

My simplistic summer lake approach worked just as well when stalking these lazy, clear rivers. Since these rivers were mainly small, and for that reason mainly neglected, the chub were not the leviathans that gave me pleasure in later years. But a 3 lb chub was a mighty beast for a not-yet teenage boy, and my 2 lb test line generally just about held fast against the mad, headlong lunges for cover of a panicked fish. Those chub also gave me an intensive masterclass in controlling my nerves and learning effective fighting tactics in confined spaces, an apprenticeship that has served me well throughout these many later years.

I had a nice rod and reel by then, paid for almost literally by the sweat of my brow: the fruits of many hours hard slog picking mushrooms as a holiday job. The rod was a Sealy 'Black Arrow', 12ft of amber glass fibre with a forgiving action, which served me faithfully for all purposes from minnows to dace, roach to tench, carp to pike as well as (some years later) barbel. It also sat comfortably in its cloth bag when lashed with baling twine to the crossbar of my bike. That old rod was one of my closest companions throughout many a long year, and I was gutted when I smashed it in the mid-1980s though I subsequently rebuilt it as a barbel stalker for which the soft through-action is ideal.

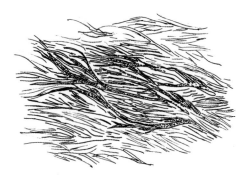

The reel was a Mitchell 308, which I had hankered after for years. It was tiny enough to sit in the palm of the hand and with the smoothest of gearings and a helical line lay that prevented light line bedding in. I still have that reel, having caught literally thousands of fish with it, though now all the black paint has lifted off with corrosion and it is more for reminiscence than use.

The Sealy, Mitchell, bike and I covered who knows how many miles of Sussex lanes and riverbanks together. No prospect was ever left unexplored, no chub unturned.

One of the largest chub I encountered in those Elysian Fields might have touched 4 lb. I don't know for sure, because I never caught it. But, for the places I fished and my tender years, it was a veritable Clarissa. I met her (that chub is a 'her' in my memory though with no objective evidence to back that up) on a baking, breathless day near a mid-channel stand of round-rushes. This particular river was a little broader than most I fished, perhaps the width of two train carriages, though the far bank was still well within the accurate strike range of my 'dipped flake' method. And dipped bread flake was decidedly the killing tactic that day, the moist crumb just waiting to be slurped into those big white lips as it hung enticingly just below a river surface dusty with grass pollen and the prolonged drought.

I must have been in a particularly relaxed mood that day, patient despite the rush of adrenaline as the lump of a chub revealed herself, repeatedly cruising in and out of view from the round-rush stand. She could have been taunting me, of course, but I am pretty sure that she was blissfully unaware of my (then) skinny, bronzed body hunched low to the bank top. And I managed to induce her to feed too on twists of flake, flicked out when she had vanished into the rush stand and there for her to discover when she re-emerged.

Judging after a little while of watching and feeding that the fish was confident enough to take a bait, I nicked some soft flake onto my hook, dipped it momentarily in the water and flicked it out across the sleepy river. It plopped lightly, perfectly in the patrol route of the gargantuan chub. I closed the bail arm, heart in mouth, eagerly anticipating.

I had not long to wait until that big, bold chub emerged again from cover, cruising into open water. She spied the bait hanging enticingly in her path, cruising leisurely towards it, and I saw the white inside of her mouth as her lips opened and then … in a split second some sort of torpedo launched itself from an unseen lie in the 'cabbage' bed beneath, straight and fast as a javelin, literally to swipe the bread from the chub's open mouth.

It was all so quick, though the memory is still fresh in freeze-frame. In truth, I was not sure what I was connected to, chub or torpedo from the depths, but I certainly knew that it was not only strong but also desperate to gain the cover of the 'cabbages' or the rushes. The soft rod flexed with each lunge though, absorbing its fight, the fact that I had hooked the fish in open water playing decidedly to my advantage.

Incrementally, the fight came to me, the peaceful river now ringed with ripples and bereft of cruising fish, as I drew my prize over the rim of the outstretched landing net. It wasn't my giant chub, I cursed my luck, but it was a pretty weighty fish nonetheless. Drawing the net up onto the bank-side grass, I gazed down in surprise. A roach! A huge one! And clearly an uncharacteristically bullish, competitive one too!

That roach pulled my rusty but serviceable Little Samson scale down to 2 lb 2 oz. It was fin-perfect, and also my first 2 lb+ river

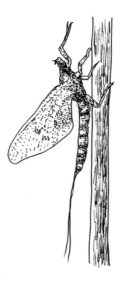

roach from a stream with no known 'form' for specimens of any species (except maybe for mullet in its lower tidal reaches).

I had no camera, no witness. So, taking a lingering last look at this lovely fish, I gently slipped it back into the warm river margin to reclaim its hidden lie in the 'cabbages'.

I was happy. Of course I was happy. But it pains me now, with older eyes, to recall that I was also a little disappointed that it wasn't the rock 'n roll experience that the bigger, bulkier and clearly hungry chub would have provided. And I never saw that chub again!

Summer roach love sweetcorn, fished 'on the drop' or using the 'lift method'

Hitching a Lift

THE CHANGING FLOW patterns of the rivers of southern Britain say much about the ways in which we have used and abused our watercourses, land and underground resources. Abstraction of water to support a diversity of domestic, industrial and agricultural uses is, of course, entirely legitimate.

However, everything in nature operates within a fine balance, and that balance is something to which we humans have paid insufficient respect in years gone by. In so doing, we have paid scant regard for the value of healthy ecosystems for all aspects of our own longer-term wellbeing.

Modern methods of intensive farming are, in many ways, technological marvels. The extent to which they have boosted the amount of food produced per unit area of land is nothing short of dramatic, and they have thereby radically enhanced food sufficiency and affordability. However, the means by which this has been achieved has sometimes had cataclysmic consequences for our wildlife, including not only farmland birds and insects but also the flora and fauna of rivers, pools and coastal seas which are the ultimate recipients of pollutants liberated by human activities across whole catchment landscapes. Significantly, this includes an influx not only of various dissolved contaminants, but also of substantial loads of sediment that choke river gravels affecting their suitability for fish spawning and the life cycles of other wildlife.

These factors are further exacerbated by the growing thirst of farming, industry and households, drawing water not only from rivers and reservoirs but also from the underground aquifers from which they are recharged. Meanwhile, drainage or surface compaction of land from intensive farming, urban development and other infrastructure denies rainfall the capacity to infiltrate into the soil to recharge underground reserves. Instead, it runs off in intense surges of floodwater, with much-reduced buffering of river flows throughout the long intervening dry periods.

As a consequence, rivers today run low in summer, with silted beds and languid waters rich in chemical contaminants from all manner of sources. The burgeoning human population, and our related demands for fresh water and production of liquid effluent, increases this array of pressures, further strangling aquatic life.

Contemporary rivers are far removed from their natural character, disconnected as they are from floodplains and marginal wetlands, and with their channels seriously impoverished in habitat. It is hardly a surprise that fish so frequently occur well below their optimal population levels and species diversity, with spawning and the nurturing of fry significantly compromised to the extent that many species are able only poorly to recruit new stock. This erodes the resilience of the whole river ecosystem, rendering it incrementally more vulnerable to predation, pollution and other pressures.

If this all sounds a bit 'doom and gloom', there are at least two silver linings. Firstly, we are at last beginning to recognise the adverse consequences for many dimensions of human wellbeing and future security that arise from continuing degradation of ecosystems, and to reconsider the implications of this in policy-making. In time, this may mean that we pay far greater heed to the wider ramifications of the decisions we make and the actions we take for the ecosystems that we need to support us into the future. Secondly, and of more immediate concern to us anglers, is that bigger fish suffer less competition for food and space when it is so hard for juvenile fish to enter the population, so those larger individuals that have managed to survive can grow to individually much greater sizes. So, whilst we may feel justifiably concerned about the prognosis for the wider aquatic and other ecosystems that support not only fish but also our own future prospects for living fulfilled lives, the potential to catch fish of specimen proportions nevertheless persists.

One of the many rivers that I fish was once a reputed trout fishery. However excessive over-abstraction of water from permeable underground strata which used to nourish river flows at source, exacerbated by the too-frequent punctuation of the channel by weirs, reduce it to a sequence of relatively static sections by mid-summer. These sections are headed by streamy water below weir pools, in which many fish species spawn, with long, ponded reaches downstream of this that are profuse with yellow water lilies but with little or no significant flow between the fishing season's start and the first notable rains of autumn.

Though far removed from its former self, this former trout stream has nevertheless morphed into a new character with a different fish fauna, including sporadic big roach which can be fished for and caught in the tepid stillness of summer.

The very notion of fishing the 'lift method' in a former trout river is bizarre, another indicator of the profound impacts of modern lifestyles on the environment. But this approach has proven highly effective in the low flows of summer. To those who may not be familiar with it, the lift method entails fishing a waggler float which, whilst unweighted itself, is counterbalanced by a large shot on the line an inch or so above the hook. Importantly, this weight must be just heavy enough to sink the float, which is set precisely at a depth that leaves merely its tip showing. The lift method was developed many years ago to tackle fickle tench that just picked up and mouthed baits without any indication showing on traditional float or leger rigs. As a tench toys with a bait presented with the lift method, it inevitably also disturbs the shot connected directly just a couple of inches away. Though often relatively heavy (generally a swan shot or more), suspension beneath the float makes this weight effectively neutrally buoyant and so virtually imperceptible to the cautious fish. And, as this occurs in the dark depths, the float rises, dances or falls over flat on the surface in response to any motion of the weight.

The lift method is inherently highly sensitive, and has been responsible for the downfall of very many tench down the years. Accordingly, it used to be a popular coarse angling method, though it has fallen much out of widespread use in the modern era. Maybe the effort of looking at a float is just too much for many modern anglers weaned on electronic indicators that stir them to consciousness only when a tench hooks itself? Whatever the reason, the reality is that the lift method has lost none of its effectiveness, and is also a hugely enjoyable way of taking fish.

Neither has the potential of the lift method for other specimen fish been lost on specialist anglers. For example, I have taken good barbel, bream, rudd and perch this way, though those are other tales altogether. But the method is also ideal for roach in the right still and slow flowing water conditions. Bill Penney, for example, was a devotee of an approach modified from the lift method, and his former 1938 British Record 3 lb 14 oz roach from Walthamstow Reservoir, together with another 3 lb+ fish to back it up in the same session, are testimony to its efficacy.

Others too, have learned that this method has its place when pursuing roach in the right stillwater and summer river circumstances, including on the summer river that I have just described.

As river flows drop off and other fish grow torpid in the heat of the day, roach can often be seen cruising languidly. They are certainly catchable and I have addressed some other approaches that have served me well elsewhere in this book. But small clusters of sweetcorn on the riverbed can often arouse their interest, both visually and chemically, whilst also having the virtue of being too tough and bulky for minnows to worry away or carry off. On such summer days, my approach is simplicity itself. Stalking the bank on 'quiet feet', wearing polarised glasses and a peaked cap to minimise glare, I watch the places where cruising fish tend most often to hold station a while or else where they pause to change the direction in which they are swimming. Then, when I see them swim off, I throw in a little handful of golden grains to pique their interest when they next pass through.

I will also be looking for other likely-looking lies, generally close to vegetation and particularly between lily leaves, where the water is deeper or is otherwise obscured. I might find and bait six or seven such swims along a half-mile of river.

In the main, the allure of sweetcorn is entirely sufficient. However, a good many years ago I found out that roach were also extremely partial to geranium oil. This shouldn't be a great surprise since geraniums and many other bank-side plants routinely shed their seeds into the river margins in the summer. The strong and distinct scent of geranium oil is extremely attractive to both roach and bream, and I have also taken barbel on geranium-scented sweetcorn. Other folks have found that adding a little strawberry flavouring to sweetcorn (often with some red colouration) can increase its attraction. I have also found crayfish flavouring to be appealing to barbel, bream and roach, but here I should add a word of warning. All flavourings are to be used with subtlety; anything more than a couple of drops of concentrated flavouring stirred into a tub of sweetcorn turns these golden grains from tangy snacks into repellent slicks. Down the years, many is the swim that I've completely killed by throwing in handfuls of over-flavoured bait. Subtlety in all things, please!

Then, with float rig set up 'lift method' style, I'll return to the first swim I have baited, stalking in low to the horizon, to see what is occurring.

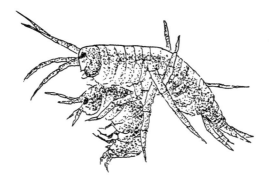

Sometimes, the fish can be seen heads-down, searching out the flavoursome particles. At other times, the water may be clouded by feeding activity. Often, fish are absent from the swim. Depending on visual clues or 'gut feeling', I will then either present a grain of corn on a size fourteen hook under the lift method, or else move on to check out the other baited swims. If necessary, I may 'freshen up' the swim with another small handful of corn grains before departing. Fishing light and mobile this way, I can circulate between swims all afternoon.

On occasion, one, two or more fish may be taken from an active swim in quick succession. They have to be played hard with the rod low to the bank top, drawing the hooked fish away from the shoal as quickly as possible, avoiding a splashy fight on the surface, and preventing a high rod tip from spooking the remaining fish.

Essentially though, this is a mobile, visual and highly enjoyable approach that rewards the persistent. ('Persistent' is a more appropriate word than 'patient', which carries the connotation of simply waiting in what may be the wrong spot!)

Over many years, on drowsy days when not a lot else was stirring in the fishy world, this former trout river has often graced me with good roach, including numerous over two pounds. Sat well back from the river's edge in summer grass, surrounded by the soporific drone of bees about their busy business and bathed by the heady aroma of moist earth and meadow blossom, I have paid just sufficient attention to the gaudy waggler tip to note the slightest knock or rise. However, with their hunger stimulated by the warm water, these summer roach are likely to pick up the corn grains boldly, causing the float to sway drunkenly and fall over flat in a bite that is far harder to miss than to hit, even when one's reactions are muted by the somnambulism of summer.

Many is the roach that has broken my summertime reveries, bucking its way to the waiting landing net to add its magnificent bronzed silver and scarlet to the blue sky, the verdant meadow and its spangled blossom, and bringing the fruity must of its slime to the already heady scents of pollen, blossom and sweet hay.

I hope that our rivers, our inheritance and legacy, can be restored at least some of the way towards their former pristine states. I would love to see them achieve this, and indeed have worked my whole life to help them so to do, recovering from strangulation by extraction of excessive water, reduction of channel habitat diversity, disconnection from life-giving marginal wetlands and floodplains, and poisoning by a cocktail of effluvia from every house, field, road and industrial site. The fish fauna too would then also be free to recover, at least as far as it is able, and that I'd welcome for the good of all wildlife and our collective futures.

This may, of course, mean that today's 'hotter' river roach spots might cease to be as they are today, as stronger flows are restored once again and the fish species of fresher currents take their rightful place. However, to compensate, as nature rediscovers a new balance, other now more static reaches would also become reinvigorated along with their populations of redfins and other characteristic fish species, as nature rediscovers a new balance.

But, whilst we wait for society to recognise the inherent value of protecting and restoring the natural and irreplaceable ecosystems that underwrite our collective futures, rather than blindly liquidating them for immediate utility or profit regardless of consequence, it is still quite possible to think our way to bigger roach in today's much-changed waters. All the more so during those times when many anglers might assume that these fish are not feeding or are not catchable, and perhaps even using outmoded but no less effective tactics not traditionally associated with river fishing.

Every season, every reach of river no matter how changed from its natural state, can be a rich oasis for wildlife, even including roach of impressive proportions.

AUTUMN
SHORTENING DAYS

2

Autumn paints a Bristol Avon riverscape

Shortening Days

AFTER THE BALM of summer, days shorten and fingers of mist rise and coalesce over the lazy river just that fraction earlier each evening. In the gathering twilight, bats feed intensely, batting lines left exposed by quivertip rods set too high over the water. By dawn, swallows mass on telegraph lines outside the bedroom window, initially in small gangs then in progressively denser gaggles on successive mornings. And then, suddenly, a dawn breaks without their nervous chatter, leaving behind just a few straggling youngsters to play catch-up on the long journey south when they are sufficiently strong and well-fed.

Of course, the year has by then been ebbing away for some time as trees reached their full leafy splendour months before, beyond which the combined stresses of insufficient moisture and too much attention from grazing and piercing insects curled and perforated their canopies. Then there was the day, weeks ago now, when the excited screech of swifts was suddenly conspicuous only by its absence, another calling card of the retreating summer. By then, much hedgerow and bankside vegetation had already withered, spent now after the crescendo of flowering.

Some days later a soft frost dusts the meadow, and then another and another, each time biting into skin and vegetation a little more harshly. And the sky furrows its brow, grey and turbulent, shedding heavy rain onto the parched land to swell tired trickles into angry, muddy torrents, ripping out soft vegetation and driving vulnerable fish fry into the less turbulent margins as the river creeps out over the bank tops.

Kingfishers struggle, not merely to locate fish fry in the murky waters but also to re-establish individual winter territories as mating pairs separate. And the fledglings of as many as three of their broods throughout the preceding spring and summer now vie for their own crucial stake on the river in battles of life and, far more frequently, death.

Stillwaters too shift their humour, reeds and weeds softening and dying back whilst the summer glut of insect larvae battens down to ride out the coming lean months.

The whole mood of nature changes with the turning of the seasonal wheel, all living things shifting gear to adapt. Roach are pushed into slacker depths and margins, stimulated to feed harder as declining length of day triggers hormonal changes that see them pack on weight across the shoulder and in their swelling roe.

These are days of transition for anglers too, as evenings shrink back, schools and other commitments resume in earnest, and centrepin reels are dusted off in anticipation of classic river trotting tactics coming back into their own.

Some roach may, in this season, appear as gilded as rudd, as pigments from rich insect and crustacean pickings accumulate into vivid fins and into a bronze-tinted mail of scales that will fade back to pearlescent silver by Christmas.

Our tools and tactics change as we seek the roach out in snatched evenings and shortening afternoons, adapting all the while to stay in touch. Then we return home where the log burner is now alight to drive out evening chills, or maybe adjourn to the light and chatter of the village pub that peeks out into the darkening, lengthening night to share and distil lessons learnt that day and to relive the rich experiences we have enjoyed by the ever-changing waters.

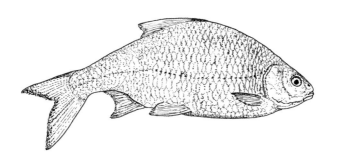

A brace of roach, each 2 lb 2 oz, trotted out two days before the season ended in
March 2008

The Weir Pool

MY FIRST EVER visit to the Bristol Avon was hugely exciting. Having moved home, leaving behind me the classic and better-known Hampshire Avon, this was to be a new chapter in my life in so many ways: personal, professional and of course, piscatorial.

Although that first trip was in late August, in my mind it is always autumn. There is just something about that waning phase of summer that feels like an English seaside town which still bears the now-faded glory of its Victorian heyday. Late summer trees may still appear full and green, but one can sense that the leaves are already drying as their goodness is progressively reclaimed into the perennial trunk. The bankside vegetation is also browning and most of the flowers have had their day in the sun. Of course, the division of the wheel of nature into four seasons has no absolute meaning. Just as one can feel the vibrancy of spring in the woodland floor even when the countryside is in the grip of late winter, so all seasons bleed across each other in an ever-changing continuum.

I don't know what it is about anglers that makes weir pools so fascinating to us. We seem to be drawn to them even at times when the fish are not. Maybe it is the rush of wind and water, sometimes deafening with their dramatic sound, or else the cleansing of the air through its interaction with cascading droplets. But sometimes the fish are there, appreciating the fresher flows, particularly when rivers are running low and tired but also when the greater depths and ripples that are often found in a weir pool offer refuge as winter frosts eliminate much other natural cover from other reaches of river.

My first ever jaunt to the Bristol Avon was to one of its many weir pools. Parking the car on the edge of a farmyard, I shouldered the tackle for the decent hike beside a tributary traversing three large fields. I plodded by under the distracted gaze of a substantial herd of Friesian cows that had raised their heads to follow this apparition in khaki, chewing cud like old-timers chomping on tobacco wads whilst observing a stranger riding through town. And then, there it was: a weir pool nestling deep in a recess in the Bristol Avon clay that a helpful fellow I had met in a tackle shop had hinted might be worth a try for decent roach.

In my first half-season on the Bristol Avon, I was to return to this well-sheltered weir pool many times. It is perhaps something obsessive in my personality that often makes me return to a new found water. Some approaches might work first time, and other tactics might do so with less success on a first encounter. Then, the new water draws me back time and again as I try to probe its mysteries, working out why something worked, or what else might have done so better. Over time, I learn the moods of the currents and the fishes, and the foibles of both in different flow conditions, seasons and times of day. A hologram forms in my mind of the bed profiles, locations of submerged vegetation, the ways these react to different flows and seasonal conditions, and the responses of fish to them. For me, that process of deduction and understanding is fundamental to my approach to and enjoyment of specimen angling of all sorts, and for roach in particular.

Homework certainly has its rewards, both in terms of fish on the bank as well as in a sense of fulfilment at their capture. That conundrum of a weir pool was to become the place from which I took my first roach from the Bristol Avon to surpass the magical, if almost entirely arbitrary, 2 lb (or if you prefer 0.907kg) barrier the following February. We'll get to the tale of the capture of that fish in due course, but it is of the explorations and innovations into the autumn and beyond that I want to tell you now. So how do you work things out in such a first-time experience on a new water?

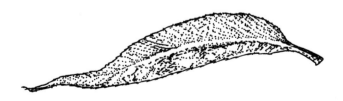

I had stalked the banks of the rather more powerfully flowing Hampshire Avon for many years preceding my move northwards within Wiltshire. My natural instinct on a river, any river but especially a strong-flowing one, is to reach for a long rod and a centrepin reel, varying the float from a heavy Avon to a stick depending on conditions. Some people consider me a traditionalist angler for this reason, but I think that this is wholly misplaced. Whilst I might enjoy trotting rivers with my thumb brushing the revolving drum of a vintage centrepin, give me a light carbon fibre rod any day rather than a muscle-straining and inherently more fragile wooden one. Furthermore, none of the people that I know who do consider themselves traditionalists would ever think of exchanging high-quality nylon monofilament for lines plaited from the hairs of horses or of virgin milkmaids (if indeed one can still find such a thing!) Although bread, which is my default and favourite bait by far, may be considered rather traditional, I doubt that the mass-produced white supermarket loaves that one buys in plastic bags would be considered so, let alone palatable, to an angling yokel of the late Middle Ages. 'Traditional' then is in the eye of the beholder, with no absolute historical reference.

So I am traditional only to the extent of enjoying traditional methods when and where they work, and due to the ease with which a good centrepin reel helps me work an Avon float down a strong current with the dropper shot and bait bouncing along the stream bed. It is certainly a killingly effective method when river conditions are suitable.

However, the flows in this new water were quite different. In fact, the Bristol Avon is virtually a set of languidly flowing canals by the summer, interspersed with weir pools in which the flows of water are somewhat quicker and fresher. And I certainly had my well-founded doubts that a Hampshire Avon float and centrepin would serve me well in such drowsy waters.

Reading the crossing currents and backwaters I recognised that, in the low and clear waters of late summer, the shattering of the surface film by constantly-tumbling water was amongst the best cover available across the weir pool as well as entraining a revitalisation of oxygen. Furthermore, the constant influx of water would be continuously washing food into this place of relative safety. One comes to realise with experience and observation the counter-intuitive truth that the slackest water to be found in a weir pool is often beneath the most troubled surface flows. So this was an excellent place to start getting to know the fish of this mysterious new river.

I tackled up with a 15ft rod, a fixed spool reel and a heavy waggler float with a long and unweighted, free-falling, tail down to the hook. Then I waded out as far as I could onto the hard gravel of the tail of the weir, threw a compressed handful of liquidised bread into the chute of tumbling water, and fired the waggler after it. Closing the reel's bail arm, winding back intermittently to mend the constantly-slackening line, I gazed intently at the float tip as it danced in the chaos of ripples as my baited hook gently wafted down beneath.

I didn't have long to wait. After maybe ten seconds, the waggler speared from sight and I tightened into a pulsating resistance. I would like to tell you that my baptism on the Bristol Avon was a mighty, arm-aching roach, but that would be untrue. In fact, it was a plump and very welcome fish of maybe six or seven ounces, the first such silvered prize to greet me from my new home river.

Sport was subsequently brisk. Clearly, the roach were making good use of the slack but well-aerated water beneath the broken surface and the conveyor belt of food, as roach after roach, interspersed with the occasional dace, came to greet me under the slanting autumn sunshine.

On this and subsequent trips, as I slowly probed and learned more of the mysteries of the small weir pool, it became clear that the 'strike zone' in which roach activity was most intense was really quite narrow. Once the float had passed out of the main splash zone, and wandered downstream to me beyond the concrete baffle on the weir bed perhaps 10ft downstream of the lip, bites were far less plentiful. And so I interspersed my float attack with quivertipped bread presented on a long tail from a cage feeder. As the feeder hit the water, the lightly compressed, liquidised bread within would burst into a tempting cloud, the length of the tail between feeder and hook allowing my hook bait to waft down slowly. Soon to be engulfed by a roach, dace or, as dusk set in and they ventured upriver into the pool, a chunky chub of up to 5 lbs.

Tightening up to the feeder as soon as it hit the water to leave a significant bend in the quivertip, the hefty drop-back bites that signalled the attentions of a fish were virtually impossible to miss even well into dusk or darkness.

I was certainly catching consistently and, with fish of 1 lb 10 oz or 1 lb 12 oz coming my way not infrequently as the autumn lengthened, I was confident that bigger specimens were there for the taking towards the back end of the season.

Of course, I was also exploring other sections of this intriguing new river, notwithstanding my courtship of this particular pool and my progressively clearer reading and prediction of its many moods. All in all, I was most impressed with my new muse, this other Avon of Wiltshire, and quickly modified my approach according to the nature of different venues and swims. One day I might break out the pole, another day the feeder, and at other times the stick float, Avon, bomb or waggler as circumstances suggested. However, this particular, ever fruitful weir pool became quite a favourite of mine in that first year on the river. Like any swim, just when you have got to know it, a winter spate scours the bed and changes the ground rules, leaving you thinking and adapting all over again. These new challenges always bring fresh enjoyment. And, as I had suspected, there was better yet to come towards the end of the season.

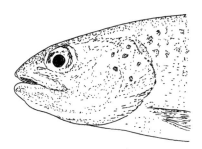

One particular dusk that first February, as colour ebbed from the landscape with receding daylight and the first stars began to twinkle through a darkening sky, my quiver tip fell back dramatically and I swept the leger rod downstream into a fighting arc. The rod bucked and kicked against the all-so-familiar and welcome 'thumping' of a big roach as it flexed its body away from the strange resistance suddenly dragging on its mouth. I could be connected to nothing other than a roach, and clearly a very respectable one. Keeping the rod tip low to the water, which tends to induce less panic in the fish and provides better buffering to reduce the tendency of the hook to pull out, I let the fish have its head under sustained pressure. Slowly, guiding it carefully, the fight came to me.

Gradually, patiently, I felt the energy drain from the struggle, and soon the dark ripples of a fish came gliding across the surface towards my waiting landing net. It is hard to know in the darkness how big a fish is, or even to discern the species. So it was not until I had lifted the net out of the water and onto the soft, dewy bank-side vegetation that I was able to slip the torch from my pocket and to look down properly at my prize. And what a prize, a plump, late-season roach, all pristine silver and vivid fins, mouthing air and nestling in the damp folds of my net.

Resting the head of the net in the water, I retrieved and zeroed my set of scales though I could already clearly see that this fish was well clear of the hallowed 2 lb threshold. Laying her in the dampened weighing sling, I took up the tension and watched the needle of the scales swing round to 2 lb 3 oz. So there she was, my first Bristol Avon two-pounder, a gorgeous fish too and not merely scraping in over the bar.

I went through the ritual of taking a set of flash photographs using a timer, but they all turned-out pretty poor. It took me many years to learn the false economy of using cheap cameras, and considerable pain in learning the lesson that all photographic equipment absolutely *must* be carried carefully in scrupulously watertight containers. The photos though were ultimately unimportant: the feeling was everything.

As I set the timer and posed with the fish, I became aware of a shadowy figure on the far bank. Though I had rarely seen any other anglers on this water, this guy was clearly a specimen hunter like myself and was trying to observe what I was up to from what he supposed was a place of concealment, having been attracted by the flash of my camera. I was in a generous and buoyant mood, and so called out into the darkness for him to come and see the fish and indeed to help me complete the photographic formalities.

Chatting to my newfound witness I learnt that to catch a Bristol Avon roach of over 2 lb really was considered quite a rarity by the river's sparse specimen fraternity back in those days. The glory days of the Bristol Avon were well known, but past. The huge, indeed unprecedented, successes that I was to enjoy in later years were yet to be revealed. And so we stood a while after I had slipped that wonderful fish back into the river margin, sharing a few secrets and stories of roach and other fishes. I met the same guy very occasionally over the following three or so years, and indeed was to put him into a swim one evening to catch his first Bristol Avon two-pounder. But that is another story again.

It is fulfilling to get to know a new water, and particularly to have successes that one feels have been earned through diligent application of the arts of location and innovation of methods to present an appropriate bait. It is a wonderful thing to make the transition from one river and set of appropriate methods that one knows very well, in my case from the Hampshire Avon, into an entirely different water and then to learn its rather different set of secrets and to come to catch on what was to become a consistent basis. My first two trips in much later years to the River Itchen were likewise to yield me four roach of more than two pounds, as the hunting instinct and the innovation of technique to match conditions yielded their own special rewards.

Constant thought and adaptation is, to my mind, the secret of consistency. One has to be forever innovating, impatient with lack of success, but considering instead how the fish are going about their lives and reacting to ever-changing circumstances. Only then one can approach a new water best-prepared to probe its secrets. And, of course, since the seasons, flows and moods of nature are ever-changing, even a familiar water is, in reality, a new water every day, every hour and with every change in light, flow and weather.

As I will tell you towards the end of this book, I was also fantastically lucky to time my arrival on my new home river just before the dawning of a 'golden era' in which a number of strong year classes of seriously big roach swam its mysterious waters. And I'll also talk a great deal more about the nature of luck, and how to help yourself become increasingly lucky.

Another chunky 2lb 5oz Bristol Avon roach brings a smile to its captor's face
during the 'back end' in March 2008

The Roach Pond

THE FIRST SERIOUS set of late-autumn frosts, which clarified the waters of local streams and pools softening their vegetation, was a signal to this adolescent roach-angler to get on his bike and pedal off to a long-forgotten pond on the edge of a secluded wood.

The pool may have been little more than a decent underhand flick across, overlooked or more likely unsuspected by local anglers. But, for me, it was a place of regular pilgrimage as much for its solitude as the fish that swam unsuspected in its dark, enriched waters.

Like the old estate lake that preoccupied the summers of my middle teens, this tiny water too had started out life at some indeterminate point as a dammed stream, the brick wall at its lower end still intact albeit overgrown and overhung with brambles. Quite what purpose it had served was, even by the early 1970s, shrouded in the mists of time. But a secret treasure it truly was.

To reach it, one had to know exactly where it was. One had first to walk or cycle a couple of miles then find a hardly obvious gap in the road-side hedge, cross a wheat field and then venture into the woodland edge. And there it lay, rarely visited, half-choked by bulrushes, but pregnant with fishy mysteries.

Drop a worm into its dark margins, and a stunted perch would be sure to engulf it. Indeed, the whole pool positively heaved with these boisterous pygmies. Rarely did one ever encounter a perch bigger than the length of a thumb, the three-quarter pounder that I banked one misty morning being a veritable ferox of a fish out of all proportion to the throng of its siblings.

There was a tench in the secluded pool too. As far as I knew, there was just the one. One fine summer's day, it was my great good fortune to haul it from the water after a lively tussle against the dense reed margin. At 4 lb, it was a pretty respectable fish for the early 1970s, and became my first fish to feature in the angling press. No one else

exposure, me and the wildlife largely took this cacophony in our stride. But one day, crouching in my quiet corner, the roar of the engines of one particular jet must have hit a precise subsonic resonance that, as suddenly and unbidden, elicited in me blind panic. In sheer inexplicable terror, I vaulted clean through the hedge, oblivious to the multiple lacerations of spines and thorns, and had sprinted half-way into the clear open space of the wheat field before regaining my rationality. My heart was a hammer in my chest, my legs and arms quaking. Even the usually bountiful birdsong was stilled to eerie silence, leaving me fearful of venturing back to the woodland fringe to retrieve my abandoned tackle.

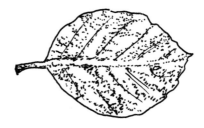

The prospect of fishing on was unthinkable after such a visceral experience, and it took some nerve and time to even cross back through the hedge into the suddenly claustrophobic menace of the silenced shade of the once so welcoming embrace of the woodland edge.

It took some time to feel at ease again by that silent pool, and in my special corner in particular, due to my body's primeval reaction honed through evolutionary conditioning despite the rational arguments that I repeated to myself inside my head. It is easy to see how ghost stories are born, fuelled by subconscious triggers of fear and dread ingrained into us as survival tactics throughout our evolutionary past, and amplified by the instinct we see so clearly in children to discern faces or other human forms in seemingly random patterns.

But I did not abandon my visits to this pool of sanctuary and, I'm pleased to say, no residual fear seemed to have lingered in the roach and other wildlife. And so tranquillity, engrossment in the natural world and sport resumed progressively as before, culminating in the eventual capture of a roach of, according to my spring balance, exactly two pounds.

Somewhere, I may have an old photo of it. More likely, it will have been lost sometime during the long and often fractured years between. But the capture of so rare a prize from such an unlikely place, tiny and reed-choked as it was, was nevertheless a significant watershed in both my fledgling specimen hunting career and my belief that I could achieve such lofty goals in seemingly unpromising and unexpected situations. A silk purse could indeed lay hidden where only sows ears seemed to reside. The capture of that roach was therefore significant as much for its physical reality as for its rich symbolism to my early and uncertain emergence from the doubts of childhood into a hesitantly forming adult identity.

As life does, mine moved on in the mid-1970s. I have no idea if the much-neglected roach pond is now silted-up, or dredged with beaten-down banks and filled with hungry carp. Or is it the same as in my memory? A shade-dappled woodland pool much loved and frequented by wild birds, woodland creatures and perhaps an uncertain child such as I was, finding their way too amongst the general confusion of adolescence while grappling specifically with the challenge of intercepting larger fish by design.

Perhaps even the roach are gone, or my tench has found a mate or had one introduced and has now filled the pool with its own progeny?

But many lessons endure. One of the most potent of them is that simplicity of approach is best. Also, that not even the most inconsequential puddle should be sneered at or passed by. And that an oasis of great peace and joy may still be found when all the world seems overbearingly turbulent. And finally, great roach may be close at hand, hidden in the seemingly insignificant places that others may overlook.

At 2 lb 14 oz and 2 lb 2 oz, this stunning brace of Bristol Avon roach warmed a
bitterly cold December 2007 day

Popped-up

THERE WAS A swim that I found one autumn where a deep drop-off had been scoured in an otherwise uniformly shallow reach of river. In full summer, yellow water lily leaves were particularly profuse in its silty depths, despite being unable to push either floating leaves or yellow flowers up as far as the remote river surface. However, by late autumn, after the first wave of frosts and spates, the 'cabbage' bed died back and softened, although the tangle of lily rhizomes remained to provide not only cover but also a rich larder of invertebrate and algal food. The roach loved it, and many is the late afternoon session I enjoyed with the waggler float intercepting large fish on sinking baits as shadows lengthened on the river surface. The roach only ceased to bite in this swim when the bats began to swoop, long before I lost sight of my waggler tip in the gathering gloom.

One evening I remember particularly well was when I lucked into a trio of roach of 2 lb 7 oz, 2 lb 9 oz and 2 lb 10 oz. I had to call on a non-angling friend as witness and photographer. This was in the days before we all had mobile phones, so I needed to net the fish carefully and then pop home to pick him up. Of course, we felt obliged afterwards to adjourn to the pub on the way back. I still have the 35mm transparency somewhere, but the after-effects of the celebratory beers with my neighbour are mercifully long gone.

That drop-off swim served me well indeed over the years until it eventually became full of silt, the holding feature vanished and the roach sought refuge elsewhere.

But, back in the day, that swim fished particularly well in spate. As with many of my favourite high-flow swims, the depression or feature against which the roach huddled was invisible through fast and coloured surface flows. But knowing the exact location of the drop-off and mat of roots enabled me to sink a swimfeeder through the quick flows of surface water into the more gentle depths beneath, and to continue to catch fish when others who knew the river less well might struggle or, more commonly, not even bother to venture out. There is, in truth, always a generous payback from hours spent angling or watching the river in low and clear water and developing, largely by osmosis, a mental map of bed and bank profiles that may hold fish when the river rises in pace, level and turbidity.

But still it bothered me where this particular cluster of roach got to as dusk fell. Did they 'turn off' and cease to feed? That seemed highly improbable. Or did the security of receding light embolden them to venture into shallower, more vulnerable waters, like barbel and dace do?

One fine autumn dusk, I set to the task of finding out, rigging up a light leger rod in addition to my waggler kit.

I had long ago found out what a killing bait popped-up bread crust can be. Back in the days when I stalked fish-depleted reaches of the Hampshire Avon near my former home near the banks of the upper-middle river, I necessarily developed a keenness for the big chub that were the most dependable specimens in those local waters. I'd often fish a rising river with legered crust, feeding handfuls of mashed bread into creases and slacker margins, waiting for a big chevin to smash the rod tip around as it encountered a piece of rough-edged crust ripped from a fresh loaf. I didn't fish delicately nor prettily, size 4 or even size 2 hooks to 6 lb line being the norm, with chunks of bread crust the size of a half-crown or even bigger 'popped-up' from a big lead on the riverbed. Bites were rarely subtle, more often just plain brutal, slamming around a full-bodied leger rod unadorned with quivertip as the fish homed in on the scent of my buoyant chunks of flavoursome bread, or else encountered them by chance at eye and mouth level in the murky water, and rapidly engulfed them.

I did OK too, with what were then regarded as specimen chub of over 4 lb and occasionally 5 lb. (This was, remember, well before the days of the 7 lb and 8 lb Avon monsters, when my chub were still considered 'specimens'!) But I also frequently had my outsized bread offerings munched by roach, and thumping big ones at that. Fish of 1¾lbs were not infrequent and 2 lb+ roach occasionally brightened a misty dusk or dawn.

Needless to say, I adapted and applied this pop-up approach by scaling down, reducing bait size to a small section of crust from the edge of a sliced loaf impaled on a size 12 hook. Though I caught many more chub, and some good dace too, roach regularly came to net using this method. As many a stillwater angler will tell you, a buoyant bait will outscore one that is fished hard on the deck every time. Perhaps this is because the fish don't need to expend energy or make themselves vulnerable by inclining their bodies downwards to pick up an offering floating at eye level? Maybe it is easier to sip a buoyant bait up without the resistance of gravity? Or could it be that a static bait just looks more suspicious in flowing water?

Back near my productive drop-off, popped-up crust on a light swimfeeder rig was certainly worth a try as bites dried up in the deeper water. As I suspected, even a tempting popped-up piece of crust went unmolested when cast to the depths. But I had other places in mind.

As bites on the float ceased, I moved my pitch upstream where currents were stronger over shallower waters adjacent to a slight crease beneath a sprawling willow. And, virtually as soon as the bait had settled, the quivertip was wrenched around as a hefty roach hungrily slurped in my popped-up offering, confident in the security of dusk. Plodding ponderously in the quicker flow, bucking against the current and jagging round the rod tip, that roach eventually pulled the dial scales down to an impressive 2 lb 5 oz, and it was duly witnessed, photographed and returned. I think it even won me a prize in the weekly angling press.

I was subsequently to learn by trial and error precisely where the roach patrolled as dusk set in, emerging from the sanctuary of deep lily roots to feed in earnest as light ebbed from the sky. Unsurprisingly, they moved first onto the run above the deep water were I had taken that 2 lb 5 oz fish, and then they proceeded to the open pool at the next bend upstream. And, when bites dried up there too, you could intercept them with a popped-up crust as they pressed further upstream along the straight above or else dropped back to the run above the lily pool.

I was to learn many times over, and to adapt that learning to many new situations, that hotspots don't generally 'dry up'. They move!

The resourceful angler will learn to move with them. On both rivers and stillwaters, sitting by habit on a known or rumoured hotspot can sometimes be a guarantee of poor fishing, or at least it may subject you to a high degree of chance if the fish are not initially responsive. It could be that the hotspot genuinely has some attractive holding feature. However, perhaps the fish only use that particular spot sometimes, or maybe it just happened that some feeding fish were passing through it one fortuitous day when you or someone else fished it.

I should just interject a caveat here that fish can certainly be intercepted and induced to feed by consistent and subtle use of free offerings when you remain static in just one swim. This is an occasional point of friction between me and a match angling buddy who enjoy fishing together. I will tend to move around all day long to locate fish and then stay in touch with them when or if they move. Steve, on the other hand, is extremely successful at drawing them to him in just one spot, match-style, and inducing them to compete for food. I never fail to learn a huge amount every time we fish together, and then to modify these lessons to add to my approach. But I'm the specimen guy, I catch the bigger ones, and that is what this book is primarily about! And, when it comes to specimen roach angling, I have found that my inherent impatience is an incredibly useful asset.

For me, a static approach to fishing in many (but far from all) situations rather ignores how larger roach behave in the wild, which you can verify for yourself through a day's fish-spotting. For much of the daylight hours, other than in quick or coloured water or in the warmth of high summer, roach shoals may in fact be relatively immobile, using cover to loaf away and conserve energy through the hours in which they are far more visible and therefore vulnerable to would-be bird, fish and other predators. Then, most frequently at dusk and dawn, their fins twitch just that little bit more as growing hunger and confidence in the lower light levels draws them out to seek food, often in the reaches where invertebrates proliferate precisely because fish larger than small fry are absent by day.

This is also frequently the time at which roach are seen 'priming' at the surface. Priming behaviour has a distinct purpose. Indeed, it has to be some sort of biological necessity as it puts the fish at considerable risk by making them far more visible and susceptible to predation. The reason that roach prime is purely down to the structure of their swim bladders. The swim bladder is simply an internal air-filled sac that fish have evolved to regulate their buoyancy. The bladders of species such as trout and perch are equipped with gas glands, which control the gas content and therefore the buoyancy of the fish. However, the swim bladders of fishes of the carp family are far simpler, developed as an outgrowth of the gut into which air has to be manually swallowed at the surface. This is why roach, bream and other cyprinids 'prime'. Therefore, seeing a fish prime also tells you that it needs to increase its buoyancy and therefore will be seeking out shallower waters. (To reduce their buoyancy, fish simply 'burp' out excess gases that become compressed when they swim downwards.) Nine times out of ten, a priming roach is moving from deeper to shallower water to feed, a gold-plated clue to both location and intent.

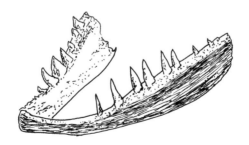

When roach start to prime at dusk, a popped-up bait presented in shallow water, whether bread, plastic corn or something else, can offer them an eye-level snack as they emerge to break their fast. Expect enthusiastic bites on lake shelves and river shallows. You can work out the best taking zones by watching the water's surface carefully where a roach has just primed, small bubbles betraying the direction in which the fish is swimming as it 'burps' out excess air to find its preferred new swimming level and associated degree of buoyancy. With practice, you may even be able to guess the feeding depth from the overall volume of bubbles appearing at the surface.

As that 2 lb 5 oz fish and many a good roach since have shown me, location is a dynamic process. It shifts over time, with river conditions and light values, and with the appetite of the fish. And those big fish can be highly mobile: I have on a number of occasions caught the same 2 lb+ specimen on successive days from swims as much as three-quarters of a mile apart.

The popped-up crust is definitely a useful tool to add to your armoury for mobile, feeding roach and for intercepting summer fish moving through warm and weedy lake or river water or else those emerging into shallower waters to feed at other times of year. Just hang on to your rod though. Despite their reputation as delicate biters, a big and hungry roach will as likely as not hit a popped-up crust just as hard as any mealy-mouthed chub!

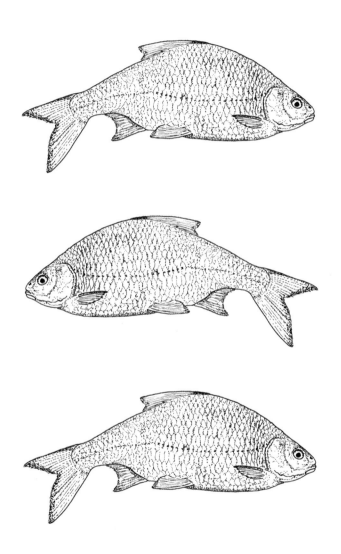

A truly magnificent specimen roach of 3 lb 1 oz taken from the Bristol Avon in early December 2011 – one of the great survivors

Last Knockings

AS WINTER BIT down on the Bristol Avon in the dying weeks of 2011, the prospects for roach were somewhat less than auspicious.

Various factions within the angling media were continuing to bay for the blood of cormorants and otters, laying almost sole blame on these perceived villains. But realities are, of course, rather more convoluted given the complexity of the environment, as indeed they are in virtually any situation in life where a scapegoat is singled out. The real danger of over-simplistic demonisation in any walk of life is that a great complexity of causative factors can be glossed over, and just as casually sanctioned.

That winter, the decline of the fishery was entirely predictable. I had counselled as much for the preceding winter in a magazine article entitled *Hard times* (*Waterlog* No.73, Autumn 2010), which acknowledged the longer-term ramifications of the severity of the preceding 2009–10 winter. Intense cold and heavy snow had gripped the county from late November 2009, with the last pile of snow in the lay-by on the top road near my home not wholly disappearing until the second week of April 2010. Winter 2010–11 was neither shorter nor any more benign; two of the most severe winters in memory coming, like London buses, in close succession after several years of milder climate.

This of course compounded other destructive influences, particularly the widespread severe trampling of the river margin by cattle and other poor agricultural land use practices. Not only were these sources of pollution but, perhaps more critically, they exacerbated the impacts of historic but pernicious harm stemming from former flood management activities which had cumulatively reduced the habitat in the river system. In a river suffering a paucity of spawning and nursery areas, the injection of new fish into the population is understandably compromised. And, perhaps more

worrisome, if we deplete the natural refuges that enable fish to evade strong flows and predation, the resilience of the whole system to a range of pressures, including the recovery of predator populations, will inevitably be profoundly diminished. And that's before we factor in the pincer effect of excessive abstraction of water allied with lower-than-average rainfall.

The increase in the numbers of otters would not of course improve this situation, though they are as natural a predatory element of our rivers as pike and perch, and so will find a balance. After all, otters were rife during those 'golden ages' of angling to which we routinely harp back, whether these be the eras of Izaac Walton or Hugh Tempest Sheringham prior to the Second World War, or when Mr Crabtree was donning his gumboots with Peter to go and 'bag up'. And the spread of cormorants is troublesome, particularly as the big 'inland seas' we have dug for them, as a consequence of our hunger for gravel to feed construction, freeze over driving packs of hungry birds to fan out and target the open water of small rivers in which fish stocks are like the proverbial 'fish in a barrel'.

So, by all means, blame the cormorants and otters if it makes you feel better, or if a single and simple hate figure helps you suspend thinking about and getting involved positively in dealing with the more complex issues and their potential solutions that can help promote fish survival and stock regeneration. But, to me, emerging conflicts between recovering populations of predators and angling interests are merely symptomatic of wider societal self-inflicted wound. And so, if we are the cause, it must surely be within our power and certainly within our responsibility to help nature recover some form of balance.

With winter 2010–11 no kinder, the adversity of a succession of two of the most severe winters in memory was going to mean that most British river systems and their ecosystems were under stress. Granted, this was not helped by more intense predation but was compounded by many other significant pressures too. The stresses of sheer survival were significant enough, but these stresses also severely compromised the ability of female fish to feed heavily enough to pack sufficient yolk into their developing eggs, without which there is no guarantee of strong survival of the coming year's spawning.

For those of us beyond a certain vintage, comparison with the aftermath of the winters of 1962–63 (the mother of all winters that saw the sea freeze) and of 1986–87 were as unavoidable as they were overlooked by those baying for the blood of more readily blamed predators. And winter 1996–97 too, when savagely cold winds turned the ground to iron, fish stocks had crashed in my local waters, clearly evidenced by my detailed angling diaries and significantly predating the spread of cormorants and otters in the Bristol Avon.

So as I settled into a swim I had cut out between two willows, leaving sufficient branches to screen it from passers-by but positioned nicely to swing a feeder into the tight gap under overhanging boughs, I was far from confident of anything of great size. The absence of competition from many older and larger fish had however allowed plenty of smaller roach and dace to prosper, and pleasure was to be found just by being there and having one's reveries periodically disrupted as a bright bar of silver made the quivertip dance.

In the *Waterlog* article, I had also noted that if a few straggling older fish were to have survived multiple jeopardy throughout the icy grip of preceding winters, including evading the hungry beaks, claws and teeth of other river life also struggling to eke out a living, they too might prosper and grow on in the absence of competition. How much of my assertion was to stoke up warm optimism in my angling soul as fortification against the harsh light of scientific fact is moot. However, the fact remains that amazing things may always be a mere nod of the rod tip away and, as they say, you've got to be in it to win it.

As dusk veiled a landscape blessed with barely a breath of wind, the blueness of the sky lightened to a pale wash framing sporadic wisps of grey cloud. I set the rod rest ready for my usual twin-quivertip dusk-time approach, but assembled only one rod owing to the tightness of the swim. No point, I reckon, hacking away valuable cover to make a swim more 'fishable' at the expense of the security it offers fish. Slipping the clasps on my tackle bag, I tipped a tub of liquidised bread into my bait apron followed by a couple of slices of fresh-sliced white bread from which I could rip chunks of flake. Then I laid out around me my landing net and other necessary bits and bobs in a familiar arrangement, so that my hand would fall easily upon them in the event of fighting a fish in the coming gloom, or as full darkness fell.

Baiting the hook, filling the swimfeeder, swinging the end-tackle out barely beyond the rod tip so it settled beneath the secure tangle of twiglets fingering the flow, I tightened down to set a slight bow in the quivertip, the betalight already faintly glowing against a skeletal dead alder on the far bank.

Fieldfares were still about, chattering in the tall oaks bordering the field, though the long-tailed tits and robin had now retreated to hunker down covertly on perches safe in the thorns into which the dusk-time stealth of the sparrowhawk could not penetrate.

The tip was not long to nod slightly, and I tightened into the thrill of silver flanks beating against the pull of river currents. A roach came to hand, perfection in crimson and silver. More roach and the occasional dace followed as light dimmed, making the hooking of bait trickier as I was loathe to show torchlight to fish so close beneath my feet.

And then, as I settled back after re-baiting and casting, the quivertip lurched round with more purpose than previously and I tightened into a solid force that kicked and kited, head-down and boring away. The light rod curved impressively, absorbing the fight of what was clearly a weightier fish as it drove outwards into mid-channel. Trout, roach or chub? I had had plenty of each from this swim over the years; it certainly had the power to be one of the many loggerheaded chub I'd banked in previous weeks.

I pondered as I held the fish on 'soft hands', barely caressing the cork of the rod butt in order to avoid the kick of the nameless fish pulling out what might have been a tenuous hook-hold but … suddenly the line fell back slack. With a familiar hollow feeling, I rewound to determine what had happened. No tackle failure this time; merely too slight a hook hold that had failed to remain in place.

Though darkness was nearly fully upon me now, and the tangle of boughs in which I had secreted myself was hardly conductive to making the best of whatever light lingered in the sky, I baited the hook one more time and cast out again. The rod tip nodded a couple of times, settling into a slight curve as the swimfeeder found purchase as I pulled the collar of my jacket tighter against fingers of chill now fondling my neck.

A couple of light raps on the tip held my attention. Minnows or small dace? But then it knocked more meaningfully before pulling round. I tightened once more into a powerful resistance, which again thumped, then thumped again, bouncing the rod tip against the flow. I knew what this felt like, but I did not dare give voice to my suspicions. Not until the hook held, not until I had seen the fish, not indeed until the caress of my landing net put all doubt to rest.

The fish kited out into the main channel, just like the previous one that had shed the hook, before driving on upstream, taking line against the backwind. I get excited, very excited, when a fish I suspect to be a roach takes line from the reel! But thus far it had headed into clear water, where I was happy to let it sap its energy with every bore and kick, only once having to side-strain it from the far bank where I knew a submerged yellow water lily bed lay unseen.

And in minutes, though it could have been hours or seconds for time has no linear nor logical flow during moments of great intensity, the fish rolled at the surface, giving me only a hint of its true identity through the gloom, but sufficient to dry my mouth and shallow my breath. Two rolls later, the fish was spent, swinging in the surface flow and, finally, over the rim of my outstretched landing net.

This fish was special. I knew that before I even felt its weight on lifting the net or peering down into its folds to see what my torchlight would illuminate.

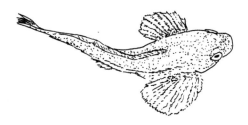

This fish was more than special. It was a true survivor of all nature and humanity in combination had pitted against it throughout more than a decade, no, probably half as much again, of survival from a tiny egg. It had endured the stresses of springtime spawning too that saw so many of the gentle giants gasp their last. Even more impressively, it had also prevailed through the icy grip of the past two fierce winters, and the hunger of so many would-be predators. This was one of my imagined, but thankfully not imaginary, straggling elders, grown bigger and fitter out of its loneliness.

Holding the fish in the net head, I wetted the weighing sling and zeroed the spring balance. This was indeed a mighty beast! I settled her into the soft safety of my pike tube, staking it securely at both ends in the slower water at the river margin, and phoned for a trusted and discrete witness to come and find me to verify the weight and take better photos than I could achieve off a monopod and timer.

As I waited, I baited the hook again and re-cast, setting the rod in the rest. But my heart was not really into the pursuit any more. I was just too excited about the unexpected yet most welcome guest pegged not a yard from my feet. I can't even remember now if I had more bites, or indeed if I connected with them. But my witness had arrived and the roach, scale and fin perfect, was verified, photographed and returned unscathed though undoubtedly wiser for the experience as it kicked off strongly into the dark flow.

At 3 lb 1 oz, or so my buddies in the angling weeklies told me, my gorgeous roach was the heaviest river fish taken all season, such was the severity of impacts right across the country of the previous two winters.

Was this a 'last knockings' in more ways than just one on this cool early December evening? And what were the prospects for the future, the remains of the season and the seasons yet to come, in the face of compounded threats and an ever-changing environment? Only being there to find out would tell.

In any circumstance, there is always hope. Despite what the doom mongers say, however dark the picture they paint, it is always worth venturing out to tempt Lady Luck to smile down upon you.

Another fine brace of 2 lb+ roach taken during a chilly March 2006 dawn from the Bristol Avon

More than a Numbers Game

SUNDAY 25TH NOVEMBER 2012 was something of a media circus, and one that got my roach radar buzzing.

My day had started at 6:40a.m., still pitch dark outside, with me doing a radio show by phone. This scheduled radio chat had planned to cover my recent book *Fantastic Fishes*. However, extreme flooding had intervened across virtually the whole of the British Isles so we talked instead about how fish react to and survive such major climatic extremes. We finished the half-hour discussion without really touching on *Fantastic Fishes* at all, so we agreed I'd be back on the show the following Sunday morning.

But that's not the media circus I'm talking about.

It wasn't until I looked out of my study window as light suffused the cool Wiltshire sky, that the dramatic state of the river valley became apparent, a sheet of muddy water spanning the floodplain more completely than I'd seen in 20 years. Worryingly, I had a TV crew on the way to do some filming for a fishing programme! So I texted Stewart, the combined camera-and-soundman, immediately to forewarn him of the situation, and we agreed that we would proceed if he could get to the village through the floodwater - but also that we would talk about how fish and wildlife cope with these conditions rather than make any serious attempt to catch anything. After several abortive attempts, Stewart eventually found a route into the village, and so I donned my waders for a fun session which we added to our growing televisual tale which was very loosely based around my book *Barbel River*, of how river life changes with the roll of the seasons throughout the year.

Stewart texted me later to confirm he had made it safely out of the village, but the water was continuing to rise as it had been when we were filming and his escape had been marginal.

But that also wasn't the media circus I have in mind either.

The circus of interest became apparent as I wandered up the field back home from the river after filming, to be greeted by my daughter belting down to find me to tell me that Malmesbury, our nearest town some five miles up river, was on national TV news headlines due to severe flooding.

Reaching home, warming cup of tea by now in hand, I went into the living room to check on the news. Many of Malmesbury's low lying older properties were indeed inundated, with people being rescued from upper story windows. The Environment Minister had also turned up to talk to the cameras of the assembled press pack. Malmesbury and its surging floodwater featured constantly on the rolling news as the morning progressed.

By now, Great Somerford was cut off, all approach roads inundated by run-off from the slopes above and from below, by surging floodwater from the overtopping river. Our plan, now necessarily abandoned with a telephone apology, had been to visit a friend, Rob, for a lunchtime curry buffet to celebrate his 50th birthday. Sad though I was not to catch up with Rob, I just love to see nature in full flowing power – in flood, wave, lightning, gale, thunder or deluge – brushing aside our arrogant cultural delusion of supremacy over such an immense life force.

This is, I think, a common instinct that unites people in some form of 'Dunkirk spirit' during extreme conditions. Indeed, as we wandered down to the village bridge to gawp at the amazing spectacle of this new Avalon of muddy floodwater overwhelming our sleepy and usually green rural idyll, and to feel and hear the low vibration and bellicose roar of water surging under the bridge arches, we merged with a sizeable crowd sharing this rare and humbling experience.

Returning home some while later, I looked again at the rolling newsreel on the TV with mixed emotions. I felt genuine sympathy, of course, for those, like our friends just down the lane, who were suffering the misery of their homes being flooded. But I also felt the itch to venture out to the river with rod in hand.

As I've said many times before, I love the 'unfishable river' as, with a little understanding of biology and a familiarity with the now invisible underwater topography of the river and its bankside, it is not unreasonably unsafe to wade the sodden floodplain and find the places in which the fish must be holed-up. But, for today at least, I had to be patient. Today, I was not only unable to get out of the village, but the pace and turbidity of the water was just a little too intense for both the fish and my own attitude to risk! Anyhow, we all know that fish stop feeding on a rising river carrying all sorts of debris, particularly when this debris includes whole uprooted trees amongst all manner of other sizeable flotsam!

Now, at this point, I should also mention that I had, for some time, been deliberately avoiding many of my regular angling stomping grounds. As I've related in the previous chapter, *Last Knockings*, the river had really suffered from a succession of extreme winters exacerbated by increased predation. I'd eked out a few roach that had scraped the two-pound mark on the season but, with my lifetime tally of two-pound-plus roach now standing at 899, I didn't want the next one to be a 'marginal two', marvellous though any large roach may be.

I was positively itching to get at the river with bread and quivertips. However, the meetings I had in my work diary for the next day would first have to be dealt with.

Despite heavy rain in the night, the river had receded from the fields by the cold light of Monday morning. I ventured out to inspect it from my back garden, and to shoot some more video footage to contrast with the film I had taken the previous day. I also ground up some bread and stashed a little fishing tackle and a change of clothes into the back of the car, before getting dressed in a slightly more 'grown up' way for the working day ahead.

My day's work was far from unpleasant – a set of meetings at the Wildfowl and Wetland Trust centre at Slimbridge – and by midafternoon I was free, stopping the car en route home in the vicinity of Malmesbury. From the pace, height and demeanour of the river visible on yesterday's TV news coverage, I just knew where a few fish might have been washed!

The river was wild, running fast, boiling, but now at least off the fields, roads and car parks, and visibly clearer with fewer leaves tumbling in the chaotic flow. Horrible perhaps to the eyes of many an angler but a glorious challenge to me!

Pockets of marginally calmer water into which fish might retreat in such high flows may be little more than eighteen inches around. And the fish may indeed be packed densely into them, pushed together into these refuges and there to be found if you are prepared and diligent enough to work many hundreds of yards of bank to locate them.

And so I set up my twin quivertips, shouldering a light tackle bag for a wandering approach with two rests and the landing net in hand and my bait apron stuffed with fresh slices and a few good handfuls of liquidised bread. No seat, indeed nothing to inhibit frequent changes of swim after just one or two casts. Owing to their need to work, burning energy to maintain station and so becoming hungry and eager to grasp any wafting fragments of food before the current whipped them away, I was sure that any fish I could locate would feed with a little encouragement.

Probing lenses of slack water on far and near banks, I worked my way along the stretch. The power of the main flow was impressive, requiring precise casting to find small slacks on the far bank then settling the rods high above the grasping flow though as often having my swimfeeders hauled away downstream by the urgent current. I could have used heavier leads or feeders of course, but the essence of this type of angling is precision casting then balancing the end rig against the flow such that any fish picking it up dislodges the weight without feeling resistance, but resulting in a huge drop-back bite registering on the rod tip. Nine times out of ten, the fish hooks itself before the strike.

Around me, the shrill cry of a kingfisher sounded regularly as it worked the river hard to secure sufficient food to see it through the cooling night. The territorial cry also spoke of incursions by intruding birds, to be located and driven off with deadly force from a territory essential for the survival of its holder throughout such challenging conditions. The violence of nature is a necessary part of its beautiful adaptation to survival throughout extreme times.

Finally, I found a fish! A big bounce of the tip was answered by the pulsating throb of what was clearly a brown trout doing battle in the turbulence and upwelling. After a spirited dance through the gyres and surges of spate water, it soon came to net, a beautiful sliver of silver spots; a lovely, fully-finned Bristol Avon 'wildie'.

Shortly, the tip of the second rod bounced back in a massive drop-back. I wondered, feeling a tremor through the rod on retrieving my end tackle through the up-welling flow, if I'd snared a willow leaf tumbling in the vortices. But no, it was a fish! A minnow dangled on my line and, after a brief admiring look, was soon unhooked and returned. Perhaps this small fish would, in turn, sustain throughout a forthcoming long winter night the hungry kingfisher that so gallantly held this territory?

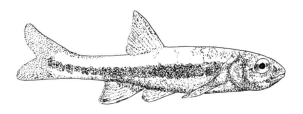

Light was now ebbing away distinctly, the approaching dusk intensified by lowering grey clouds shedding light drizzle. But we were now in the 'witching hour', so gathering together sense enough to give up and go somewhere warm and dry was just not going to happen!

My final swim was tight, to say the least: barely a sliver of marginally slacker water hugging the far bank against the otherwise rapid push of wild, twisting currents across the river channel. Precision casting was essential, the feeder bouncing ineffectually downstream unless placed within four inches of a far bank beneath which, I knew from prior experience, a slight undercut could hide a fish or two under overhanging grasses.

As I was recasting the second rod one more time following two abortive attempts to find the right spot of calmer water, both times the end tackle summarily swept aside by the ferocious river, the tip of the right-hand rod fell back abruptly and I tightened into another twisting, turning fish that tussled across the flow. Soon, another fit little wild-spawned brown trout nestled in the folds of my landing net.

Three fish from an 'impossible' river! I was most pleased!

And then once again, as I prepared to recast the second rod, the tip of the upstream rod fell back abruptly in an impressive drop-back as a fish bolted downstream in the fierce current. I felt it kick and roll, a roach at last? It bucked in the flow as I lowered the rod tip to water level. And soon, a pristine silver and scarlet redfin was nestling in the safety of my net. How fantastic to bank a roach of perhaps fourteen ounces in such adverse conditions!

Casting again as the light ebbed away, I was rewarded by another roach even bigger: this time, perhaps a little over a pound. A real monster in the circumstances, it warmed my heart as the cool, dank dusk and fading light seeped into my fingertips.

All of the fish that came my way in this tight swim fell to the upstream rod. It is strange how fish always seem to favour just one of the twin quivertips on any given day.

Bang! The tip of the upstream rod fell back again dramatically, and I tightened into solid resistance as a fish kicked back against my steady pressure, rolling this time on the surface in the nearing dark before hitting the fast paced flow.

I used the push of water to my advantage, rod tip held downstream, low to the boiling surface, winding line back as the fish was pushed downstream. And soon, what was clearly a solid fish was gliding, ready for the net, in the narrow strip of marginal slack by my feet.

I reached for her and she slipped over the net rim on the first offering, a fabulous fish, all scale-perfect pristine silver with gloriously rosy fins. I cradled her in my wetted weighing sling, raising the whole on zeroed scales, and watched with bated breath as the needle settled.

2 lb 2 oz!

A fabulous fish! Granted, not the most massive roach I'd ever seen, held or caught, but it was a perfect one, and on an 'impossible' day.

It was also number 900!

All this on a day when merely being out was itself a challenge, getting a bite a triumph, and catching anything at all absolutely miraculous. But to bank a magical 'two'? My 900th 'two', and all? I was truly elated!

Slipping the fish back, wishing it well, I fished on for a bit. I even banked another roach: a much slimmer fish though of impressive length, of around a pound in weight. But the day was already perfect, and the night was now upon us. I was more than content to pack up and make the short trip home to bore my long-suffering family rigid about it all around the log-burner!

Will I ever top one thousand two-pound-plus roach?

I do get asked that from time to time. But, honestly, who really cares?

I frankly doubt I'll ever hit that somewhat arbitrary figure. The number itself is significant only for the amount of zeros in it, much as many prophets of the end of the world have used such groundless portents to predict the apocalypse at the turn of the millennium, or have done so and no doubt will continue so to do at the turn of pretty much any randomly selected century or decade. My pessimism about attaining this largely random watermark is not only due to my age, but also to the recent but sustained malaise of our rivers allied with my aversion to venturing forth to 'bag up' in known specimen stillwaters.

More importantly, when numbers take over from appreciation of these fabulous fish, it is time to sell off the tackle and do something more worthwhile!

My own lesser target met, maybe I really will fulfil my annual perpetually broken promise to go and spend some more concerted time trying to catch specimens of a few more species.

More likely, I suspect, I'll continue to be infatuated by the thought of those glorious red fins.

And, who knows, maybe one day I may even catch another over the magical 2 lb mark?

WINTER

THE BACK END

3

Extremes of weather do not necessary signal an end to productive fishing but
demand adaptive thinking

The Unfishable River

THE DARK CLOUDS scudded overhead, seemingly brushing the tips of the trees as they were driven fast on a blustering westerly breeze. The river had risen after the successive rainstorms of the past two days, stable in height now but brown, turbulent and creeping out through the bank top vegetation into the meadow hinterland. Though warm, at least for the season, the day had driven the dog-walkers indoors, and the word 'unfishable' had been uttered more than once as friends phoned me at home during the morning to ask how the river looked and to discuss piscatorial prospects.

Perfect! Give me a high and coloured river in winter and I will venture out in thigh waders whistling a jaunty tune. I do realise that this is the sort of behaviour to endorse the prejudices and preconceptions of non-anglers, and to perplex more than a few fisher folks besides. But to me, an 'unfishable' river signals the very best prospects for really big roach.

So let me tell you a tale of a three-pounder from one such supposedly unfishable winter river. But first let me talk of the guarded chat that happens between like-minded specimen anglers.

We are a funny breed, us specimen roach aficionados, keen to chat in hushed tones with those other rare folks equally in thrall to our particular passion, yet reticent on precise details. In part, this is to guard the huge investment we will each have made in locating big fish, but also because we really don't want to suss out too many of our colleagues' secrets. After all, to feel you have poached a fellow angler's fish is to deny yourself that special sense of fulfilment in having earned your prize. If I wanted numbers of big fish without that type of effort, I would spend my time using proven techniques at the known swims on known waters, but that just doesn't appeal to me at all. I realise that my view is from the relative luxury of having a solid track record of big roach. It remains true however, that the 2 lb 1 oz roach I took on my first ever visit to the River Itchen, on quivertip as a heavy frost settled into darkness, was worth more to me than many considerably larger fish later taken from more tested swims on familiar rivers. The detective work is everything and the rewards, even the small ones, are all the more richly to be savoured.

Now a discussion with a trusted angling buddy (a singular type of creature that I'll tell you about in greater detail elsewhere in this book) is, in many ways a remarkable thing. If there is someone you fish with regularly and with whom you share information freely, you will recognise some of what I have to say. Conversation between you will turn to a particular reach of river and, as you talk, you will make a mental journey together through every bend and bankside eddy, cattle drink and outcrop of brash, overhanging hawthorn and run between decaying rush stands. As your minds travel in synchronisation down the river, pausing to explore each submerged mat of lily roots and unseen drop-off in the riverbed, you discuss notable fish landed or lost in seasons past and the conditions that brought you and the fish together in that fateful encounter. And you realise how encyclopaedic and three-dimensional an image you have constructed in your mind of the watery world that so captivates your attentions.

It is this holographic understanding of the river's profile, and of the response of current and fish to this understanding, that comes alive when the river is 'unfishable'. Watercraft, your reading of each boil and backwash, forms a precious amalgam of knowledge accrued from observations at other times of the year, emerging as an instinct about likely lies. Even when the water is running hard across the meadows, you will know where to wade to find the familiar but now unseen river edge, and cast with confidence into raging water knowing that your swimfeeder will fall into an oasis of slack water beneath. This is fishing at its most intuitive, most demanding. But the big roach are burning up energy and so must feed hard, and also with much-reduced suspicion as natural food is swept into secure, dark waters where fish may have little or no time to inspect it before it is swept away. The fish will then take baits not only the whole day through, but also quickly and firmly.

Hooking a heavy roach in these conditions is fun too. Bites are rarely subtle, the quivertip curling round determinedly, your strike finding the solid resistance of a fish that seeks fast water flank-on to kite and kick as hard as any white-lipped chub. Then, bringing a wide-flanked redfin to net across quick and turbulent surface water is sure to test the nerves of even the most chilled angler, as rough and crossing currents grab contortedly at net, fish and perhaps tenuous hook-hold alike.

Sometimes, when the water level is not so high, you may find a quiet corner to sit. Then, sheltered by alder or blackthorn scrub, explore the features of the pool in a more leisurely way, concealed as much by your immobility as by the cover of vegetation So hidden, you may even enjoy the sight of a kingfisher working hard to glean a living of small fish from the cool and dirty water. Or, as the light ebbs from the late afternoon sky, you may hear the small birds around you break into an excited warning twitter, alerting you to the approach of the sparrowhawk. Perhaps you'll feel the wake of turbulent air as the predator strafes close along the bank of herbage. Or watch in fascination as a late-winter pair of sparrowhawks work as a team, one trying to flush out a thrush from the security of a thorn bush whilst its partner waits, patient as death, to lunge in the unlikely event that the worldly-wise songbird falls for that old trick.

The short winter afternoons pass by all too quickly as you probe each slack and overhang, seeking to discover their well-kept secrets with swimfeeder or float. One fish here, none in other likely lies, two or even three there. Maybe you will search two miles of the river, far from the car park where you lack nothing but human company. If you bank a particularly large fish, or perhaps a sumptuous brace or trio, hold your catch in the soft mesh of a pike tube staked at both ends in a slack while you wait for a trusted buddy to find you as witness and photographer. A pike tube is more forgiving to fins and skin, and its dark fabric relaxes the fish more effectively than a keepnet which is anyhow too cumbersome to carry. But, in the main, you are your own company and witness because the 'numbers game' matters far less than the hunt, the capture and the appreciation of a beautiful fish on a dull winter's day.

Alone, but never lonely, your attention is periodically diverted upwards by the whistling of a passing flock of fieldfares or redwings, silhouetted against the cool sky as they wing their way between berry-bearing hedges on either edge of the floodplain. Stalking the river's edge quietly, you could surprise a heron, the grey fisher paddling away on broad wings, cursing you with its hoarse 'grumpy old man' cry. Or a shy water rail lurking in the margin of softened reeds may sidle surreptitiously into deeper cover on your approach.

One such afternoon, I had worked the river diligently. The 'Bush Pool' looked particularly attractive. My buddy and I called several kinks in this reach of river by that same name, Bush Pool, as all were undercut on the outside of the bend and overhung by bushes. Perhaps we just lacked the imagination to give each a different name. However, despite their identical titles, we always seemed to known intuitively to which Bush Pool the other was referring. (We also talk without confusion of two different 'Fence Pools' on this same reach of river for similar albeit hardly mysterious reasons.) But this particular Bush Pool was far from rewarding today. In fact, I was about to have one last cast before moving on when a movement upstream and to my right, caught my eye.

Right in the middle of the fastest, most turbulent and shallow part of the run that fed into the Bush Pool, right where big roach would never be expected to lie in spatey water and right where there was no sub-aquatic drop-off or any other feature to break the fierce flow, a really big roach top-and-tailed, unmistakably silver and red. What on Earth was it doing there, and priming too?

Fortuitously, as I was just about to re-cast into the pool, I was able instantly to alter my swing to cast upstream, immediately above where the fish had topped. The quivertip bounced as my swimfeeder rolled across the riverbed, finding a toe-hold and releasing its load of liquidised bread to tantalise any roach into taking the large lump of flake on my hook.

The rod tip had not settled into a firm bend for more than four seconds before it sprang back determinedly, and my sweeping strike downstream set a fighting curve throughout the blank. The fish bucked, but the pressure from down-current meant that it could gain no purchase to resist me in the churning water. Perhaps unceremoniously, but using the advantage of the angle of my light quivertip rod to the flow, I pumped the fish away from the nearside overhang of canary-grass and the decaying remnants of a round-rush bed in mid-channel, and led it into the deeper, largely snag-free water of the main Bush Pool.

There, the fish stayed deep, plodding then kicking, but light pressure from above kept it in open water where it could not weed itself. By the weight of each buck of the rod, it was clearly a very heavy fish. Nevertheless, the advantage was mine so long as I played it gently to avoid pulling out what may have been only a tenuous hook hold.

The fish bored and drove, seeking to run, but each time restrained by the vertical pressure which put it at a substantial mechanical disadvantage. Within a minute or so, the broad flank of a plump roach rolled at the surface, its mouth gasping in a mixture of air and water as it slipped towards me and finally over the frame of the outstretched landing net. I lifted the net head to cradle this wonderful fish in the soft and secure folds of netting. As I drew it to the bank and lifted the net frame from the water, I suddenly realised that this fish felt far heavier than I had anticipated. And, as I settled it on the moist grass, I was amazed at both the depth of its chest and its width across the shoulder.

The light was still good as I watched the fish pull the wetted weighing sling down past 3 lb, finally settling at an impressive 3 lb 1 oz.

How do you describe the psychological impact of a roach of three pounds or more? I've really no idea what words could even come close to capturing the literary breath-halting moment that you sight one in the flesh, as instantly brain-stopping as experiencing a full solar eclipse or the ground-shaking reverberation of sudden and unexpected thunder close overhead. The sensation in the head is as profound as a first kiss, baffling expectation or even imagination. It defies the senses in ways that are quite literally surreal, that something so familiar can be of such extreme dimensions. And, make no mistake, even though a gigantic roach may be dwarfed by even a modest carp in physical bulk, a big roach still looks absolutely huge.

The fish now in my hands may have been, I think, my ninth or tenth roach of 3 lbs or over at that time. But, like accidentally biting your tongue hard when chewing a tough steak, that instantaneous involuntary gasp is in no way muted by familiarity. This winter spate specimen may not have been my biggest ever, not even my largest from this river, but it was downright huge nevertheless, for any three-pound roach is more of a mythical beast than a mere 'specimen'.

I didn't fish on, or at least not straight away. First of all, I stowed the fish gently into the pike tube and staked it down before phoning my buddy to find me and help with proceedings. Once the fish was safe and secure, I then sat down on a log washed up on the bank by the previous flood and savoured the moment.

The river gurgled gently and the ragged clouds bustled past above the jagged tips of bare oak trees opposite. Senses heightened by euphoria, I took pleasure in the texture of the early leaves of celandine by the water's edge, darker green and smoother than the sparse new blades of grass poking skywards between them. I enjoyed the manic dance of decaying round-rush stems in mid-stream, juddered by the urgent rush of water. And, as if orchestrated that way, a swoosh and clack of wings from directly above alerted me to a small flock of tufted ducks flying low and fast and banking tightly. Though I was familiar with the sound of wings scything air in a tight turn upon sighting a concealed angler at the last second beside a favoured pool, these particular diving ducks were behaving rather differently. As I watched, they were travelling fast and low, changing direction by the second. I scanned the sky beyond them and, sure enough, the small, swept-back profile of a peregrine was shadowing their movements high, high above. Their fascinating and strategic dogfight switched and turned, the cut of air from the tips of banking wings fading into the background rush of wind and water in motion as the ducks carved a switchback path downstream and out of sight.

No day to hurry this, nor any longer one to allow the daily drama of the living river to pass by unappreciated.

Time passed by pleasurably, unhurriedly, until my buddy arrived. Then, after we had weighed the fish, taken and reviewed the photos, shaken hands and watched that incredible beast vanish into the muddy waters with a flick of its vivid fins, we decided as light faded from the lowering sky to drop into a couple of swims in the mile or so between the Bush Pool and the car park. A few fish came our away, but the spell weaved by the presence of that red-finned beauty remained with us as a palpable inner glow. No need for words or idle chatter. The hunger for a further river giant was sated for now.

We had been in the presence of something magnificent, a mythical beast revealing itself from the hustling flows of the surging winter river, and one that had clearly failed to read the books about how big roach are meant to behave or where they should swim, and clearly also be feeding, in a swirling winter spate.

Remember that as you scan these and other pages for definitive words of wisdom!

A fit 2 lb 5 oz Bristol Avon roach nestles securely in the folds of my landing net

Under the Ice Sheets

WINTER 2009–10 BIT down hard. The village school closed after excessive snowfall, once before and again after Christmas, making the journey for teachers and children alike hazardous. Pipes froze. Stillwaters froze. The birdy predators that had grown fat on them in summer and autumn suddenly found themselves cut off from their man-made feeding grounds and descended on the remaining open moving waters in their droves, hunting in packs with ferocious efficiency.

The river fishing was hardly productive. Although I had huge fun casting a fly for pike, not much else was feeding and it was unsafe to venture beyond those waters that I could reach on foot. Instead, the wood-burner performed sterling work keeping our little house warm, and afternoons were spent with my daughter and other kids from the village on the toboggan run of a steeply-sloping field at the end of our lane. Moments like this are too special to spend casting unproductively into a clear and largely fishless river.

And then, the following winter of 2010–11 bit down even harder. Two successive harsh winters that were quite exceptional for the south of England decimated the fish stocks. As snow enveloped the landscape in early December on that second big winter, the countryside was a dangerous beauty with black ice in every dip and straight. No-one seemed to be catching anything, or even venturing out. The rivers around where I live seemed pretty much dead as this new wave of severe cold and predation compounded the legacy of the previous winter.

It takes quite exceptional circumstances for me to abandon my beloved rivers during the winter months. However, these were exceptional conditions. So, perhaps counter-intuitively, it was to the frozen stillwaters that I decided to turn my attentions, and to quite remarkable effect.

Some miles from where I live is a complex of gravel pits, and it is to these that I headed once the snow had cleared sufficiently to allow me to do so safely. In previous years, I had learnt some of the moods of these large still waters in cold conditions. To my advantage was a little understanding of hydrogeology (the underground movement of water) and so I was able to ascertain the likely flow of groundwater into and out of these lakes. Groundwater, flowing through underground strata, is one of the reasons chalk rivers can be so productive throughout the winter. Heated by contact with underground geology, these groundwaters can reach the surface at some 10 or 11°C, which is considerably warmer than ambient air temperatures normal for that time of year. This is why chalk rivers will often be seen to steam on a cold day. And an influx of groundwater into a stillwater, particularly through porous strata such as gravel beds into which extraction pits have been dug, can have the same effect.

I had noticed in previous years that ice formed more thinly in certain areas of one particular lake, precisely the area where I expected the groundwater inflow to be at its strongest. Also, I had found previously that I could locate roach there in even the most bitter of conditions.

And so it was to these stillwaters that I turned my attentions, using simple though adapted waggler tactics. This entailed a pair of 15ft float rods, one of which was fished with a sliding float rigged for 'lift method' tactics, in order to read the bed profile. Using this approach, I found what I was looking for: an underwater drop-off where the lake bed dropped from five to seven feet. I was able to position the slider float rig on the edge of this drop-off, fishing at depth but also serving as a range-marker against which to cast my other standard, slow-sinking waggler set-up. Both wagglers were thus settled around two rod-lengths out, with a chunk of bread flake popped up from the bottom 'lift method'-style and the other free-falling amongst sporadic small handfuls of liquidised bread.

Fish, you see, respond not so much to absolute temperatures as to changes in temperature. They can acclimatise to stable temperatures both high and low. However, even when conditions are warm, a declining temperature can turn them off. Conversely, warming water can stimulate feeding and, if you can find a marginal zone warmed by groundwater, you may just find feeding fish in the most inclement of conditions. Certainly, the fish that I was to catch were not cold to the touch as I lifted them from the landing net.

As important, or perhaps more important, was that each float was resting right up against the floating shelf either side of the channel I had smashed in the marginal ice. And although detached ice sheets created problems from time to time, the fish were eager for my bread baits after only about twenty minutes.

My match fishing buddies are in agreement with this point – fish can feed hard under the relative security of an ice shelf when bites can be simply impossible to find in clear cold water. I believe this is because fish feel safe under cover, yet they feel exposed to bird predators where there is clear water overhead.

It is amazing what a little watercraft and consideration of fish biology can do to help you 'get lucky' in seemingly hopeless conditions; my baits were descended upon by hungry fish on a day, indeed a whole month, on which I had this large water body entirely to myself. Seemingly, no-one else thought that fish could be found feeding.

What followed over the two-hour session on that first snow-bound day was my most remarkable stillwater session to date, accounting for fourteen roach in all. Each of them was 1 lb 14 oz or more and, incredibly, half were of 2 lb or more (two at 2 lb 0 oz, two at 2 lb 1 oz and three at 2 lb 2 oz). All were in perfect condition, benefiting from almost total neglect on a water that unaccountably seems to attract only carp and tench anglers in warmer months. All also fought really hard in the clear water. It was simply crazy that I had such silver fish potential entirely to myself. I wonder how many other of our heavily-fished stillwaters, where only carp or tench are angled for using fairly unsubtle tactics, have equally untapped redfin potential?

I could have fished-on had not a low bank of cloud swept in taking out the light and bringing with it a blizzard. Once the 'white-out' descended with its full ferocity, I simply couldn't see my floats any more and so had to pack up well before dark.

Though I may be a river man through and through, this experience encouraged me to try a few other stillwaters whilst the rivers were in such poor form. And so I experimented on other neighbouring pits too, catching a few roach here and a few there including fish beyond the 2 lb barrier when the river was simply not fishing, and other people were not out fishing.

But could I ever hope to emulate that stillwater best day?

The grip of frost and snow did lift briefly and I was back on the river for sporadic sessions and a very few specimen roach. However, the impacts of predation had paid a heavy toll on the river's roach stocks, and the remaining fish were not only few but also well underweight in the food-poor, chilly waters. And it was the stultifying impact of a series of hail and ice showers that drove me back onto the stillwaters which were mainly still frozen from before the festive break.

Arriving at one of the gravel pits one early afternoon, after a morning of heavy frosts that had frozen puddles and garden ponds solid and whitened the grass, there was nevertheless a continuing thaw as the ice shelf broke rather easier on a down-wind corner.

Again, I fished paired waggler rods with bread flake on the hook, trickling in a loose feed of liquidised bread to maintain a cloud in the water column adjacent to the ice shelf and above the lake-bed drop-off. I knew from experience that the roach tended to patrol there, perhaps again due to a slightly warmer influx of groundwater. Also, like the pre-Christmas session, it took a half-hour or so for the roach to home in on my bait. But then bites came regularly up until complete darkness. I switched to black-topped floats as the light faded in order to present a decent silhouette into twilight, but the coming night eventually forced a halt to proceedings altogether.

The net result though, by the time I packed up as a heavy frost formed around me once again, was a stunning net of a dozen roach all of which were 1 lb 14 oz or over. The best of eight roach of 2 lb or more went 2 lb 3 oz. Not bad for an evening on a largely iced-up stillwater with rapidly-dropping temperatures leading to another big frost. This was yet another personal stillwater best bag of chunky roach on a day that had seemed so hopeless. Also, another day when, once again, I seemed to be just about the only person mad enough to be out fishing across the entire county!

Luck plays a large part in our capture of fish, but so too does a degree of watercraft and consideration of fish biology. I still marvel that no-one else bothers to fish these productive lakes for silver fish. I was to enjoy more bags of large roach with a few fish to 2 lb 5 oz by the time the thaw set in for real, waking up hoards of small stillwater roach that swarmed onto my baits long before the bigger fish could find them. By then though, the rivers were fishable again.

But still I feel I have not yet tapped the true potential of these large and mysterious stillwaters.

One cold day perhaps. One cold, cold, day …

Specimen dace and roach are often found and sometimes caught together in
deeper refuges when the river pulls hard during the winter

The Magic Triple

THEY SAY THAT lightning doesn't strike twice in the same place, though of course it is highly likely to, given the right lightning conductor. Three times is even less probable, though the odds can again be narrowed when a prominent point that is well earthed presents itself. The analogy of lightning striking twice is often extrapolated to other circumstances in which chance plays a hand, including fishing. However, the same principles apply, a good grounding in watercraft and a high point of awareness of how conditions are affecting fish in their feeding habits can prove more attractive to that kind of lucky lightning.

One cold February evening I had the very great good fortune to suffer this kind of triple lightning strike: the only known one of its kind.

One of the many things that we owe to Richard Walker is the term 'Magic Double'. Walker used this to describe what, in his view, was one of the pinnacles of angling: the capture of a roach of two pounds or more and a dace of a pound or over in the same sitting. It has been my great good fortune to have landed six Magic Doubles over the years. The biggest dace tend to hang in deeper waters with roach on the back end of the season before they rush up to spawn on shallow shingle runs, and so it is that many have fallen to me on roach fishing forays.

There are occasions when one simply wants to go and catch a fish. The late afternoon of the evening in question was one such when, after a fortnight of snow and hard frosts, the Bristol Avon had been stripped of colour with the fish lethargic to the point of almost complete torpor. However, as we know, when the temperature is stable for a long time, however low, fish will acclimatise. On this particular day, despite a biting wind, the air temperature had just lifted fractionally for the first time, and it struck me that this could maybe bring some fish on to feed.

Keen to catch at least something, I powered down the computer early and headed for a deeper stretch of the river where I had often found fish willing to feed in quite cold weather. Whether this was because the fractionally deeper water offered better cover, for it was certainly more green and mysterious than the shallows around it, may have been a contributory factor. But for whatever reason the fish there always seemed to be more willing to take a bait than on pretty much the whole of the rest of that reach of river.

Evenings were still short, and so this was a session snatched from the jaws of looming darkness. I didn't set up a float rod with the gloom already gathering in, but instead took two light quivertip rods each equipped with fine line and feeders to present bread flake over liquidised bread.

Arriving at a swim where the riverbed dropped away beneath an overhang of willows and a raft of twigs and other litter, I settled myself down on the bank, arranged my gear around me and then dropped one of the feeders into a likely-looking nearside eddy.

My suspicions about the effects of the rising temperature were right! The quivertip banged around almost immediately and I struck into a lively roach of a few ounces. On a bitter evening, after a prolonged fish drought, such a brilliantly silver and red reward is a joy to behold.

The fish were in a feeding frenzy, guts empty from long enforced inactivity yet hungry from their expenditure of energy fighting currents and also the hormonal signals to feed intensively in preparation for the coming spawning season. The slight rise in temperature had pulled a trigger impelling them to feed, feed, feed.

I didn't even have time to get out my second rod and fished on with just the one quivertip, to bank roach after roach in sizes from 'razor blades' to over 1 lb. The roach were feeding as if after an enforced famine, and I too was loving every fish after my own famine of bites in the preceding week or so.

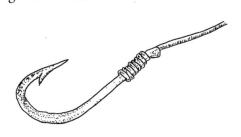

As the light began to ebb away I got more adventurous. The streamy water under the far bank looked promising and so I loaded up my swimfeeder with crumb and made an exploratory cast. The current was distinctly stronger here, carrying the feeder a little way downstream before it found the riverbed and the rod tip dropped back. I closed the bale arm and settled the rod in the rest with just a slight bend in the quivertip.

The dusk was encroaching fast. Were it not for the biting breeze, wisps of mist would have been rising from the river. We were entering the 'witching hour' when the bigger roach start to prime and feed. Without warning, the quivertip kicked over and I struck into the gyrating resistance of a plump dace. It was a gorgeous fish of around a dozen ounces, adding its unique spice to the substantial bag of roach I had already accrued.

I put a fresh pinch of bread flake onto the hook, filled the feeder once again, and cast into the faster water. Like the roach under my near bank, some impressive dace were lined-up eager to intercept this welcome food in the faster water.

To cut the tale a little shorter, a string of substantial dace came to join me on the bank and I was having tremendous fun. Then, I tightened into something that put up a slightly more solid resistance. It didn't fight with the angry head shake of a chub, the surge of a barbel, or the kick of a roach, but in a series of excited tremors. I played the mystery fish carefully on soft hands, and soon she was in the net. I gazed down at the unexpected but very welcome sight of a great big female dace, heavy with spawn, which pulled the scales right round to exactly 1 lb!

Slipping her gently back in the water, for I had no keepnet and would anyway not have retained a fish so ripe with spawn, I fished on. Sport, both beneath the rod tip and in the far bank run, was undiminished as I swung in a succession of roach, dace and the occasional gudgeon. So unexpected in this biting cold, so enjoyable; I was having a glorious time.

Then, as the colours of the far bank lost their intensity in the waning light, I bent into something that was considerable less keen to come to the net. I bided my time, exerting a forgiving pressure as the fish thumped and kited, betraying its identity through the language of its dance. In a couple of minutes, clear to see even through the gathering gloom, the flank of a hefty roach glinted as it rolled over the rim of my outstretched landing net. At two ounces over the magical 2 lb barrier, it was a truly big fish, and bigger than any I had caught from this stretch of river for a decade. Notwithstanding the coming spawning season, the roach was in fact quite 'hollow'. It also had the hunched appearance of an old fish, but also had begun to form the characteristic head nodules of a male roach in spawning livery. I speculated just how heavy this fish would be were it in peak condition. I slipped this venerable gentleman back into the river with a nod of my fishing hat, wishing him well, and thinking that I had only a few more casts left before the darkness drove me back to my fireside.

A 1 lb dace and a 2 lb roach: another Magic Double! My fourth by my reckoning at that time, and when the river was so low and clear that no roach angler in their right mind would expect such good fortune.

I cast again, this time short and into the nearside swim from where the 2 lb roach had just been taken. This was more as a 'wind-down' from a fun session than with any serious intent or expectation. But, as the light was nearly gone, a speculative strike at a circumspect nod of the quivertip was greeted by the brutal thud of a chub shaking his head in temper somewhere down in the dark water.

I held on tight, seeking to maximise the advantage of surprise which is often a key moment in the first split seconds of a fight with a big chub. Through the gathering gloom, I scanned the dark water to see where this fish might bolt. The raft of debris downstream was an obvious refuge, and we all know how adept chub are at jamming their heads into snags and either smashing the line or shedding the hook. I was able to keep it out of the debris though and sapped its energy as best I could against my light tackle whilst it was still fighting out in the relatively clearer water in mid-river. Slowly, very slowly, I felt the fish begin to tire against steady pressure.

As the fight came to me, and the fish fought higher up in the water, I extended the landing net handle fully and offered the net head to the chub so any panic reaction would be more safely handled away from the detritus of the river margin. Predictably, the chub bolted, straining towards the flotsam down below me as I swung the rod low to the water's surface and exerted maximum side-strain from upstream. This was going to be tight!

Fortunately, my calculation was just about right, just about, as the chub swung inches short of the raft of debris. It bucked and bored, each lunge answered by the flexing of my light rod, but each also arching it a little less precariously. After a long moment of the heart-stopping anxiety that we all know so well, the chub at last rolled on the surface, took in a mouthful of air which nearly always signals the end of the fight, and then wallowed heavily into my outstretched landing net.

With slightly shaking hands, the fish still held in the net head in the river margin, I zeroed the scales for the third time. Putting the chub in the weigh sling and taking up the strain, I watched the needle pull round to 5 lb 4 oz. This was a very respectable fish from the upper Bristol Avon!

Gently, I carried the weigh sling to the river edge and slipped the fish back. There really was no need to cast again. Just as one rarely hankers after a dessert after a fine main course, I had had my fill of good fortune. Instead, I simply sat in quiet satisfaction, watching the cold evening gather in around me as the amber and purple fingers of dying sun rays painted cloud layers in the far western sky.

What a memorable session. But what was the name of this remarkable bag of fish? Well, there was none, for I knew of no precedent. So, borrowing and adapting from Walker, I christened it a 'Magic Triple'.

Of course it was not planned. It was neither expected nor justified in the circumstances of a quick dusk session snatched on the edge of a bitter river. Furthermore, it is not something I expect to replicate even in perfect conditions. No, just plain dumb luck once again, and of the kind that is not meant to strike twice, let alone thrice.

And so I reflect even now, with a warmth belying the chill of that 'magic' night, on that special trio of platinum bar, red-finned perfection and bronzed flank. A Magic Triple indeed!

The stuff that legends and dreams are made of:
a somewhat younger author cradles a 'river best' of 3 lb 6 oz 4 dr trotted from
the Hampshire Avon in March 1992

A Hampshire Giant

THE FOUR-AND-A-HALF YEARS I spent living virtually on the banks of the Hampshire Avon opened unprecedented angling horizons, deepening my appreciation of the wonderful and diverse water life that has captivated me and formed a central theme for my whole life. However, they were also years of angst. Some facets of this need not trouble us in this book, but others were self-generated through the unhealthy obsession that I developed in my pursuit of a three-pound roach throughout much of my early thirties.

Let us be quite clear about this. A 2 lb roach is still regarded as the 'fish of a lifetime', at least for the average angler. Those that apply themselves diligently will narrow the odds of that chance encounter. But a three-pounder … now that is a whole different ballpark altogether.

It is true that there is now a handful of stillwaters, generally well-known, from which largely known fish can be had using scaled-down carp tactics. But for the generality of waters, a three-pound roach is beyond rare. Catching one is indeed about as realistic a goal as finding a wild unicorn.

I know of three-pound roach on several rivers and a few less widely-renowned (and consequently less expensive) stillwaters. That itself is the first trick of 'location'. But finding out where they are at any one time, identifying the baits on which they may be induced to feed at the specific times they are feeding, and presenting the baits to them in a convincing way that is also sufficiently sensitive to detect their bite is another matter entirely. Big roach do not grow to great sizes because they are gullible. No, big roach have seen it all, and their wariness is rightfully a thing of legend. So, to pitch oneself headlong into the pursuit of such a prize from a wild water is a sure-fire recipe for madness!

And so, notwithstanding the successes of those Hampshire Avon years with big roach, barbel, pike, dace and other species, my self-judgement of my apparent shortcomings in failing to bank a 3 lb roach opened the door to all manner of inner demons. I most strongly advise you not to take yourself down that particular path to madness!

Life moved on and I moved away, and with it my dream of - no, my craving for - a three-pounder receded as other priorities took over. The irony is that it was only on a chance visit to the banks of the Hampshire Avon near Fordingbridge, having moved away some months before and not expecting too much, that fate smiled.

I am trying to look for a positive way to describe it, but to be quite honest the weather all day had been foul. The gale-force westerly wind, though warm, had driven horizontal rain up the river into every slight gap in my tackle bag and clothes, whipping the river surface into deeply-troughed waves.

I was confident that the swim I had selected had potential, though presenting a bait to any fish that might be within it in a convincing way was going to be quite a challenge. I ruled out a legering approach straight away, in part because spotting a subtle bite when the wind was buffeting such an exposed spot would have been impossible but also because trotting a heavy float from a centrepin just feels the right way to tackle a river of this nature.

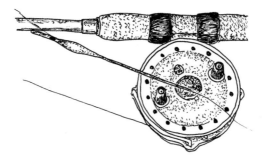

I made up my 15ft rod, attaching an old favourite centrepin and threaded the line. The wind and waves were serious, so my choice was a bulky loafer float that would carry five swan shot. I needed the float to resist the current and wind, but also to be able to hold it back in the strong currents at the water's surface so the bait could trickle along the riverbed, beneath the BB dropper shot, at the more languid pace of that deeper flow. As many people know, I prefer to use a black-painted masonry nail rather than a string of bulk shot, and this I attached to the line using two sections of rig tubing. A foot or so below this I tied a loop in the reel line, attaching my BB shot above it and linking a 12in hooklength and a size 12 fine-wired hook. Thus prepared, I was ready to brave the howling gale and the rain that drove under the rim of my hat and into my face.

From mid-morning onwards, I trotted that heavy loafer float persistently along a deep bankside run, feeding in handfuls of mashed bread in the hope of drawing a late-season roach to my bread flake hook bait. All day I persisted, rain spattering my glasses which made bite detection all the more tricky.

It is rare for me to flog the proverbial dead horse. Rather, if I can't induce the fish to feed then I am impatient to find where else they may be feeding, or at least may be induced so to do. But I had a feeling about this swim: it just felt 'right' with the river in this condition, although I am certain that I could have found somewhere rather better sheltered from the elements. So I trotted on, cast-after-cast held back by thumb pressure on the drum of the centrepin to inch the float down the crease, handfuls of mashed bread dropped intermittently to stimulate hunger. As the day waned, I was certainly getting hungry and hoped the fish might begin to feel the same way.

By now, the light was fading from the sky, encroaching darkness bleeding the colour from the riverside vista. My float was a black dot, increasingly hard to discern as it rode the heaving checkerboard of troubled waves. Very soon, I'd have to pack my float rod away and I was unsure if I'd be able to fish on due to the uncertainty of spotting a bite on a quivertip in this howling wind.

But then the float dipped. There was something purposive about that dip, not fierce but self-evidently no casual drag through soft weed.

My thumb arrested the rolling drum of the old centrepin and I swept the rod back upstream in a gentle strike. I felt a solid thump, then another, then a third. Something very solid was attached to the end of my line, something that was sending familiar signals through the cork handle into my hand. Then, as a big roach will do, I felt it roll, and saw a substantial boil on the water's surface in the gloom downstream. I dropped the rod tip close to the water's surface, letting the water buffer the forces as I knew from bitter experience that a light hook hold can easily pull out when a fish rolls like this. And then I felt a very solid thump one more time.

Something slow and ponderous was fighting back, yielding me no line despite my sustained pressure. I knew then and there that this was a serious fish, and my heart was thumping just as much as the fish was thumping back at me on the other end of the line.

Time slows in these moments of high drama. I recall thinking to myself again and again, 'Don't come off! Please don't come off!' The fish meanwhile bore towards the near bank, taking line freely from the centrepin. But I most certainly did not want this leviathan to weed itself, extending my 15ft rod outwards as far as I could to side-strain the fish as hard as I dared. In that suspended eternity, I felt the pressure on the line and hook build, rod and fish momentarily balancing each other, and then the unseen monster veered away from the undercut bank, kiting out into the river channel. To my great relief, the thumping and rolling fight resumed in clearer water.

The fish would take line from me … and then I might win a little back. When a roach takes line, you just know it is a serious fish. Or had I latched into a bream? Or a hybrid? Or perhaps even a chub that was playing tricks on me? There is nothing quite like the fight of a big fish to raise all manner of doubts.

By now the fish was perceptibly tiring, so I readied the landing net. Not having been sure what I was going to fish for in this unpredictable weather, I had packed various bits of kit, but only the one landing net. This was my vast 40in pike net, which was proving a complete nightmare to manage with my left hand only, as it was alternately wrenched by the gusting wind and the strengthening current.

A pair of anglers who had been fishing further down the bank came wandering up to watch the action on what for them, as indeed me up until this single bite, had been an entirely fruitless day. They had already started to pack their gear away and had a long drive back to London ahead of them. We chatted as the dogged fight continued … was it bream, roach, chub or hybrid? Then the fish rolled just in front of me. A roach then. But not just any roach … it was colossal, certainly the biggest that I had ever seen at that time. Or was it part-bream?

Despite the many big roach under my belt by that date, the thrill of catching another, and particularly a real 'biggie', just never dulls and neither does the anxiety one experiences during a tenacious fight when all may yet be lost in a moment of ill fortune or lack of foresight. My heart pulsed seemingly in my throat.

I turned away a kind offer to help me net it. I have always netted my own fish so that I have only myself to blame if I cock it up.

Another roll, and the fish was nearly spent as it turned again towards the riverbed, but still I loosened thumb pressure on the rim of the centrepin to avoid losing the fish on a last-minute panic dive. And, at the next attempt, she rolled over the drawstring between the arms of the gigantic net. At last, she was mine!

It was dark now as I hauled the net onto wet grass, and three pairs of eyes peered down into its folds. The fish should have looked tiny, dwarfed by the disproportionate dimensions of the pike net. But it didn't. It looked big. Positively enormous in fact, and every inch a roach. None of us said anything for a moment, gazing down and trying to take it all in. After many years catching big fish and witnessing many more, I had never clapped eyes on anything quite this enormous.

And then we burst into manic laughter, shook hands, and nattered away inanely like excited schoolboys. The weighing and photographic procedures were dealt with smoothly, for which my witnesses were invaluable. We took particular care to ensure that the key features of the fish could be verified later in the photographs. But this was a true roach, no mistaking. And, at 3 lb 6 oz 4dr, a fish of such serious proportions that none bigger was taken from the Hampshire Avon, and (I think) the whole UK, that season.

The good old traditional method of a hefty float, held back in strong currents by a long rod and centrepin reel to enable the bait to trickle at an ambling pace on the riverbed had proved its worth once again. A personal goal had been met, but as is the strange nature of fate, only after I had given up on its pursuit. The red-finned fever was at long last broken.

Back in my days of madness when living on the banks of the Hampshire Avon, one of the more successful anglers had offered me the somewhat frustrating tip that: 'After the first one, they seem to get easier.' And so it has proved in the intervening years. Whether it is the self-belief of having 'done it', the reduced levels of anxiety with which one fishes, or just plain luck, I pass this tip on to you too with all my best wishes!

But the best advice I can offer is just not to ever expect to catch one of these 'wild unicorns', for down that road madness most certainly lies!

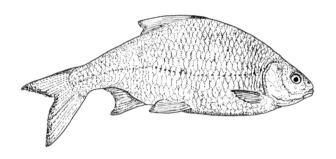

My 450th 2 lb+ roach, a lovely 2 lb 7 oz fish taken from the Bristol Avon in
January 2007

Poor Old 'M'!

BORN AS I was in the 1950s and cutting my specimen teeth from the late 1960s and into the 1970s, I suppose I can be forgiven for staying loyal to the wisdom imparted by Richard Walker about the hunting of specimen fish by design. Other than match fishing, the predominant angling pursuits in those days were almost entirely casual. The hooking of large fish and the far from predictable consequence of actually landing them was, in the main, regarded as a matter of luck.

Richard Walker changed that through both his scientific approach and the eloquence of his communication, both substantial contributions to our branch of the sport that are hard to overestimate. But my adherence to the 'location, bait, presentation' mantra is far from slavish. As I see it, the very notion of pursuing big fish without having first done all one can to determine where they actually are and then when they may be induced to feed is nonsensical, or at the very least subjects oneself to an irrational level of randomness. Then, of course, one turns one's attentions to the appropriate bait and the optimal methods for its effective presentation.

As author of a fair number of angling books and magazine articles, and a regular contributor to radio, TV and other media, I have tried to share as freely as possible the lessons I have learnt that help me catch big roach on what seems to be a more consistent basis than many. My tips on tackle and its modification cover much of 'presentation', always of course explained in the context of the water conditions to which each is applied. As regards 'bait', I have also shared lessons learnt, including those underpinning some dramatic successes but also the inevitable abject failures. And about 'location', I have also tried to be as open as I can about watercraft and the thought process, scientific principles and 'hard yards' on the bank that distil it, through years of diligent pursuit, deduction and observation, into a matter of instinct.

However, I rarely, in fact almost never, tell anyone other than my close angling buddy exactly where I catch my fish. This is not meanness on my part so much as safeguarding the fruits of my considerable efforts. Better anglers will understand and respect this.

One such 'better angler' is a friend that I shall refer to simply as 'M'. Now, I had known 'M' for some years, a tench fan of some renown, but he suddenly developed 'the hots' for a big roach. We used to chat occasionally on the bank or over the phone about where and how to intercept them. However, though a capable angler, 'M' just seemed to be not that blessed by Lady Luck when it came to roach. Of course, as a seasoned angler, 'M' understood that 2 lb+ roach would not simply jump out of the river at him because he'd expressed a general desire. However, after a couple of seasons of frustration, 'M' finally picked up the phone and asked if he could accompany me on a roaching session. Enjoying his company, trusting his discretion, but also swearing him to absolute secrecy, I eventually agreed.

We met over a cup of tea in my kitchen one lunchtime in late February to discuss prospects and approaches. The day was cool and overcast, the river carrying a little colour and height, and our spirits were certainly boosted by that auspicious constellation of circumstances.

Knowing that 'M' was keen not merely to bank a big fish but also to learn and earn any redfins that came his way, we considered and agreed a plan of attack. This entailed dropping by a stretch of river from which I had taken 'low twos' in times gone by but which, for whatever reason, I had largely neglected for a couple of years. The spates of intervening winters and an increase in trampling by cattle had changed the shape of the water somewhat, so I really didn't know what to expect. This would be as much a journey of exploration with fresh eyes for me as it would be for M, to whom the water was entirely new. What better way for us both to learn and earn?

The top boundary of the stretch was a decent yomp away, but the water here was streamy and the residual submerged vegetation provided cover attractive to roach. 'M' set up an Avon float rod and trotted a likely-looking run between residual weed beds, whilst I dropped into the bend below where the water had carved a slight

drop-off in the bed before running under an awning of overhanging willows branches. I think that we both started on bread, though M may well have been on the maggots. After half-and-hour, I'd had three chub to about 3 lb, the bigger ones giving me a robust and brutal battle on light stick float tackle as they bolted to the overhang of willow boughs and submerged roots. I also was rewarded by a plump and plucky roach of about half-a-pound. 'M' had a bite, but bounced the chub on striking.

For the following couple of hours, we worked our way down the river, probing likely looking lies with float tackle and a sparse loose-feed of bread. Talking through the pros and cons of each potential lie, swim selection was a personal choice for each of us though we fished close by to stay in touch. We fished them all, an undercut bank or raft of sweet-grass here, the lee of a patch of winter-softened round rush there, a promising drop-off, a chute of water past remnant beds of yellow water lilies, runs beneath trailing willow boughs, a nearside eddy into which an alder tree had fallen some years before remaining only as a wooden skeleton. Each and every one offered cover, food and the promise of a roach or two. I managed to winkle out half-a-dozen more plump roach to around one pound and four more chub to about two-and-half pounds, as well as the odd dace and minnow. However, fate was smiling less sweetly on 'M' who, for all his efforts, remained biteless. I was beginning to feel for him, though he remained cheerful and optimistic.

I did have a plan of sorts in my head though. This entailed us reaching the slow and deeper water above the weir downstream as the light began to fade. To have crashed our swimfeeders into the run too early would have been to potentially scare non-feeding fish, and would be as likely to have driven the minnows into a feeding frenzy before they receded to the margins as the gloom and predators encroached. And so we arrived in a state of high expectation.

Settling down together, breaking out our seats and quivertip gear, 'M' and I compared notes. He adapted his rig to more or less to copy mine. Broadly similar quivertip rods and reels loaded with 4 lb line aside, this similarity involved attaching small cage swimfeeders to swivels on a boom of nylon, the swivel then running within a loop tied in the main reel line. To this, 2½lb hook lengths about 15in long were connected loop-to-loop, and size 12 fine-wired, micro-barbed spade-end hooks were tied. Similarly rigged, we filled our swimfeeders with liquidised bread, baited our hooks with fluffy white bread flake, and cast out to see if any roach were home.

They certainly were. After only a couple of minutes, my quivertip curled round, and I swept it off its rest into the characteristic 'thud' of a large redfin as it turned side-on to the current. The fish was strong, thumping against the resistance of glass fibre as my soft quiver rod bucked to absorb its lunges, the reel's ratchet now switched off to enable the fish to take line if necessary and so soften even further the impact of its struggle on what might have been only a slight hook hold. 'M' watched as the roach came slowly to bank, slipping over the rim of my outstretched landing net. I dropped the rod back onto the rest, both hands now on the net handle to draw the fish safely up to the bank top. And there she lay in the soft folds of netting, cushioned by soft grass moist with a slight dew in the encroaching dusk. 'M' and I peered down at this apparition of silver and scarlet, 2 lb 2 oz of Bristol Avon treasure, fin perfect and hooked fairly in the lip. The fish were clearly on the feed, so we slipped her back a little way downstream and resumed our efforts.

This time, I suggested 'M' cast exactly where I'd just taken my fish. Intent on helping him to his first specimen redfin, I packed my feeder again and baited my hook, casting it casually upstream out of the way, landing it close to where brambles cascaded into the river margin. I tightened up to put a bend in the quivertip, all the better to spot drop-back bites. 'M' asked for my advice on how best to bait up and, when satisfied he'd got it right, he swung the end-tackle out into the gentle current with an easy underhand lob. We were sitting close together now, both willing his 'tip to curl around.

You can probably guess what happened next …

My quivertip fell back dramatically and, instinctively, I reached for the rod butt, sweeping it low to the water to take on a fighting curve against solid resistance.

Thump! Another decent roach by the feel of it. I maintained pressure with 'soft hands', using the added advantage of current to absorb the fight of the fish and to draw it inexorably down river towards us. Ask any of the more successful specimen hunters and they will tell you that, no matter how many sizeable roach one catches, that 'heart in the mouth' sensation never leaves you. And so, mindful also of a fallen branch on the river margin between us and the fish, I played it cautiously to the net rim and the safety of the enveloping mesh.

Once again, I laid aside the rod as 'M' and I gazed down into the moist netting. Another pristine fish, plump and bigger than the last one but as perfect in colour and detail. The scales settled at 2 lb 5 oz. Hands were shaken. M was pleased for me, but clearly a little frustrated at the inertia of his own quivertip.

Slipping the fish back into the river a little downstream again so as not to disturb our feeding shoal, we discussed how best to use the twenty or so minutes left until full darkness and the predictable 'switching off' of these Bristol Avon roach.

We decided to revert to 'Plan A' and sat together with me dropping my bait immediately in front of us and M swinging his slightly downstream. But this time, I baited up his swimfeeder with my own liquidised bread, put my own bread flake on his hook using whatever scents were on my hands … hell, those were the only differences between us!

In the next 15 minutes 'M' at least had a bite to miss, so things were looking up! Meanwhile, three more smaller roach, two dace and a chub succumbed to my rod. This was all the more inexplicable as we were using identical baits and kit just a yard or so apart.

Now, 'M' is a laid-back kind of chap and genuinely happy for others' successes, but it was all getting a bit much for him. So, as the darkness enveloped us like a tent, conversation turned to which of my bottles of beer to open first when we got back to the wood burning stove which would have by now been lit, and was throwing out its inviting warmth into the living room.

However, Lady Luck was to deal us one more loaded hand.

My quivertip pulled round decisively and I swept the rod back one more time into a sprightly resistance. It felt more energetic than the other fish, and I speculated that it might be another chunky chub so 'M' wound in his tackle to avoid tangles as the fish took line.

It is easy to exaggerate in the retelling the fight with a good fish, and to over-dramatise the power and intent of its runs and the skill of the captor in overcoming its purposive force. However, the reality is generally far more prosaic, the switch from patient attention into intense reaction dilating time from seconds into fragments of eternity. But the fish nevertheless fought well, the thumping resistance making it progressively clearer what exactly was connected to the end of my line. And, in another indeterminately-long moment, the silvered beauty slid across the now dark river's surface towards my waiting net, like a fragment torn from the moon's reflection.

We didn't re-cast. We didn't need to, as the experience felt complete. We did, however, weigh the fish, probably a male, at 2 lb 1 oz.

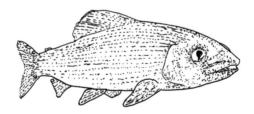

This was a more than respectable bag of fish including a trio of two-pound roach to me, but sadly only two tentative, missed bites to 'M'. How, or why, is that even possible, let alone fair?

Philosophically, we discussed the lessons learnt as we broke down the rods and shouldered tackle bags ready for the decent tromp off home, and an even more decent ale to round off the day.

Crossing the head of a weir on the long march downstream, I acted on a whim. We just had to have at least one cast into the dark, churning waters as I felt sure that roach in this lower reach of river would have migrated upstream with the dusk to feed. M was happy just to sit and watch, so I unfixed the rod bands from my quivertip set-up, baiting hook and feeder from the scraps left in my bait apron, and swung the tackle out to where I knew the rush of dark water calmed on meeting a rising bank of shingle.

The feeder settled, quivertip bouncing a couple of times before coming to rest in a gentle curve. The pair of us sat back, both intent on the isotope whipped just beneath its terminal ring. The tip juddered with the play of crossing currents, each of us reading the tales it was spinning us. And then it pulled round firmly, decisively, the curve extending down the light rod as I bent into a solid pull. The fish bored, using the current well to kite to the left as I maintained pressure, dropping the rod low to the water's surface. As it reached flows of a steadier pace, I felt the characteristic bucking as the fish turned side-on to unaccustomed resistance, flexing its body away to break free. The rod arched to its rhythm, progressively drawing it closer now to the waiting net. Closer and closer. And then …

The line fell back slack, the life that had suffused the glass fibre blank sublimating away like a spirit passing from a corpse at the end of a life.

That visceral, deflated sense is never dulled, no matter how many big roach one has caught. I knew just what I had been connected to and had lost. Though of course we may all nod in intellectual agreement with Isaac Walton's declaration that a fish has never been lost if it has never truly been won, the stark reality is that the term 'gutted' is never applied to a more apposite situation.

There may have been more feeding fish out in the dark waters. In fact, we knew that there almost certainly were. But, for both of us, our appetites for beer and warm food, fireside and time with family, were suddenly far more pressing than those for more roach. And so we broke down and shouldered our tackle once again, trudging back homeward across dark meadows in an introspective mood.

We warmed up once indoors, both figuratively and literally. The magical elixir of decent beer, a plate of warm food, and the relating of our experiences to my better half in the glow of burning logs worked its healing magic.

The lessons we have experienced about the vagaries of fate, even when I'd used my own baits and hands to help 'M' place his tackle exactly where I'd been pulling out fish, were unusually opaque that night.

As 'M' left for his journey home, wisely but reluctantly declining more of my fine ale, his final confiding remark to me was that he was quietly, if guiltily, pleased that I'd 'dropped' that last weir pool fish. A fourth 'two' on the bank when he had failed to hit just two tentative bites might just have been too much to bear!

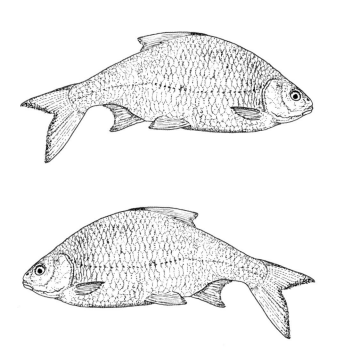

The Bristol Avon river record, a chunky specimen of 3 lb 2 oz trotted with a waggler under stormy skies at dusk in March 1994

A River Record Tale

WHAT DOES A river record mean? Well, not a lot really. It is certainly not a recipe for enduring fame and fortune. But it does set a relevant benchmark against which to understand the local potential of waters and also the relative merits of the fish you catch from them.

Going back many a long year now to March 1990, I had the great good fortune to catch a whopping great dace from the Hampshire Avon that pulled the scales down to 1 lb 4 oz 8dr. My witness and I decided to round this down to 1 lb 4 oz, thinking that the British record was an ounce or two heavier. On returning home, I found out that the British record at the time was in fact 1 lb 4 oz 4dr! However, since we had agreed on the bank that the dace was 1 lb 4 oz, we were not going to go changing our story. And so the British record was never claimed, although that fish still holds the Hampshire Avon river record, as well as the Ringwood and District Angling Association club record, now nearly a quarter century later at the time I write. If you want to read more about this and other big dace catches, go read my book *Dace: The Prince of the Stream*, as this *Redfin Diary* concerns itself mainly with roach.

Then, on moving northwards to the Bristol Avon, I suddenly found myself with some new and relatively unexplored waters, at least from the perspective of their specimen potential. To say that I was pleased with what I discovered would be an understatement. The Bristol Avon is a far more intimate river than its larger Hampshire namesake to the south of Wiltshire. (Very little of the Hampshire Avon is in fact in Hampshire; owing largely to county border changes many years go, far more is in what is now Dorset though most is, and it has always been, in Wiltshire so some call it the Wiltshire Avon.) But I thoroughly enjoyed my voyage of discovery on this more bijou northern cousin over the subsequent years. I have rather lost count now, but I think that I hold, or have held, river records for eight species from the Bristol Avon. From eels to tench, dace and even carp, I fished for many species (and caught some by accident) with huge enjoyment.

But the first of my river records from the Bristol Avon, and the one I most value, was a roach. It is the tale of its capture that I want to relate to you now.

It was another tempestuous day in North Wiltshire. Sadly, it was also a working day. All day long, I had watched the glowering sky through the office windows, rain spattering against the glass and merging into great droplets that ran down in cascades. In fact, not a bad day to be indoors all in all.

My car was parked outside, the boot full of tackle. However prospects looked pretty poor as wave after wave of rain clouds, driven on a fierce breeze, swept low overhead dumping their loads of moisture onto the saturated cityscape.

Nevertheless, the end of the season was approaching, so out by the river I would be when released from my duties. I kept looking at my watch, subconsciously preoccupied and planning for what lay ahead, counting down to the time when I could escape the air conditioning for the wet and stormy outdoors. And, at last I was free and firing up my car in record time.

The river was over twenty miles distant from the office but I made up that distance at something a little less than reckless pace. Soon, I was pulling on my waterproof layers and shouldering the tackle. As I had driven, light had been slowly dying in the sky, whilst clouds continued to speed in from the west on gusts of wind that were thankfully not too chilly.

The river had responded as I had expected, up and brown with a pronounced surface chop. But these are the conditions in which the larger roach can be stirred into feeding, particularly this late in the season, so I approached my twenty minutes of remaining visibility in an optimistic frame of mind.

In seconds, I had released my ready made-up waggler rig from the rod bands, electing this approach for its numerous advantages. Intuitively, a float is always best when the river is pushing through, allowing me to cover and search the riverbed to intercept any roach that may be feeding. On some gusty days though, a float that is attached to the line top-and-bottom can be a disadvantage as zephyrs catch and drag the line, compromising presentation. Conversely, a waggler float, attached bottom-end only, can allow me to sink the line between float and rod tip and therefore to evade the clutches of the wind and surface drift.

My waggler approach is hardly subtlety personified. In fact, it draws criticism from many for its apparent crudity. However, in essence I like to under-shot the float grossly in order to leave at least a couple of inches of long and bulky peacock quill sticking out of the water. Unsubtle though this may appear, when I fish it over-depth, it allows me to not only hold back the rig against the current but also to allow the float to pull the dropper shot across the profiles of the riverbed. So most of the time the float is fairly well dotted down, and its rise and fall tells me a great deal about the bed structure and, of course, any attention that my bait may be attracting from fish. I've caught many big roach this way, so can live with the criticism of others!

This particular evening I fed handfuls of liquidised bread down the inside line, tight to the bank which I knew to be undercut. Putting a large piece of bread flake on the hook, I released the waggler, allowing it to swing out into the crease between fast midstream and slower bankside currents, holding it back tight to trot down the stream.

Bites were pretty quick to materialise. Indeed, they needed to be in such a short dusk session. My first three casts yielded two roach, each of them over one pound. And then, as the light had all but vanished, rendering my float nearly invisible, it dragged under and I tightened into solid resistance. I leaned upstream, feeling for movement, wondering if the hook had embedded itself into one of the lily roots that I knew were thick in my swim. And then the 'root' kicked back, and kicked hard, kiting out into mid-river and taking line as it did so. It certainly felt like a roach, kicking and bucking against my steady pressure, but I could not be certain beyond the fact that this was a solid and large fish.

I side-strained the fish upstream, rod held well out from the bank but also with the tip low to the water. Swinging the tip down to water level can be important when fighting a big roach, as indeed with many other species of fish. Fish seem far more perturbed by pressure coming from above the surface, perhaps as an ingrained reaction to the threats of predator birds. And a less agitated roach will panic less and so reduce the chance of the hook pulling out. Sometimes, in a tight fight, I will even plunge the rod tip well below the water surface and often this enables me to lead the fish towards me with relatively little fight, a useful ploy when they are heading towards a snag. Thus led by sub-surface pressure, they sometimes remain relatively docile, at least until they get sight of the landing net!

Responding to my pressure, the fish rolled, as big roach are wont to do, before diving back down and running for the middle of the river. I gave the fish its head, my reel back-winding against slight thumb pressure on the spinning bail arm. When a roach runs, it is rarely a tiddler. I knew that this was a special fish.

As the strength ebbed from the fish, its muscles progressively tiring, I was able to gain a little more line and lead it towards my waiting net. However, the fish was far from spent, and it is always a period of particular great danger when a roach is still fighting hard against a shortening line. As the fish approached me, it kicked right, diving for the undercut bank. I had to lean out as far as I dared, applying outward pressure from the fifteen foot rod to strain it gently away from the tackle-hungry raft of canary-grass roots. The roach's final lunge now spent, the fish wallowed at the surface, turning on its side, and at last I was able to draw it into the safe embrace of soft mesh.

Putting down the rod, both hands now on the landing net head, I lifted the fish softly onto the moist grass. It was huge.

Fortuitously, the farmer, who was a good friend, had come down to see how this mad angler was faring on such a wet and generally horrid night. Even more fortuitously, he had a big feed bucket in his hand, having just fed his heifers. This we filled with river water and carried the fish into the relative refuge of a field shelter. And so he was also on hand not only to weigh and photograph the fish for me, but also to share a special moment.

That fish, fin-perfect and plump, thumped the scales down to 3 lb 2 oz. A whopping great roach.

After admiring it for a brief while, we carried the bucket back to the river. There, after a brief moment of reorientation, the fish kicked off strongly for the turbid depths, never to be seen again. However, none the worse for its experience, I am sure that it spread its strong genetic heritage into the next generation as the roach massed upstream for spawning a little over a month afterwards.

A roach can live up to a dozen years, exceptionally reaching 15 or (though only once from scales that I have personally counted) 17 years. That fish was a true veteran, surviving all the perils that befall a silver fish such as a roach throughout its life. More than half can be expected to die as eggs before even hatching, and then the emerging fry are preyed upon by fish, insects, birds and all manner of predators. As a roach grows on, pike, perch, eels, chub and trout can feast upon them, as can larger roach and other 'non-predatory' species of fish as well. Cormorants too, and herons, dabchicks, kingfishers, otters, mink and all manner of other predators. And that is before we even mention the huge variety of diseases to which roach and other small fishes are susceptible!

A roach of 1 lb then is a huge and very rare fish. Two-pounders are true leviathans, which have struggled and survived against seemingly overwhelming odds. What can one say about a three-pounder? They are simply impossible, and they look improbably and exquisitely big too. That special fish would have died long, long ago by now. However, it lives on in my memory in its full brilliant red and pearlescent splendour. It does so because it was simply a magnificent creature, but also because it happened to be the rod-caught record for the Bristol Avon. It remains so twenty years later.

I have equalled that roach record twice, taking two different 3 lb 2 oz specimens from the same river, and have of course exceeded it on other rivers and stillwaters. I've seen far larger fish too, including two different specimens of around 4 lb on the Bristol Avon that my angling buddy and I stalked in successive summers and even had feeding right under our rod tips, albeit to no avail. But that first river record roach remains special.

But it is only a river record. It is there to be beaten, one day. Perhaps, like the Bristol Avon river record dace, it might be me that smashes my own record. Perhaps not. But, who cares? It is, after all, only a benchmark set at a fixed point in time.

But, to me, something so extraordinarily beautiful will always be far more than just a benchmark.

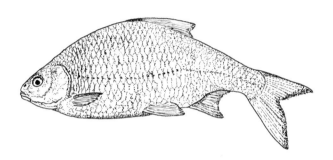

A unique shot? Eight 2 lb+ roach including a 3 lb 1 oz giant caught from the
Bristol Avon at dawn on a March 2007 morning

8x2x2

THE CLOSING WEEK or two of the river season, so eagerly anticipated the whole year through by anglers of a certain red-finned persuasion, can go out like a storm when the river is right. However, these weeks can just as often, or perhaps even more frequently, ebb away with barely a whimper. In our modern landscapes, over-drained in urban and rural areas alike, water is no longer held in damp floodplains, diverse riparian wetlands, nor the moist substrata of river valley rocks and soils. The precious fluid instead speeds on seawards in spates of heightened intensity, bearing with it eroded soil and all manner of pollutants down channels straightened by drainage engineers particularly since the 1940s but often many more years beforehand.

So when the flood abates rivers now quickly decline to low levels and lower flows, no longer able to clear silt from life-giving gravels and weed beds. And, when frosts clarify the water, the roach scurry for any stick of scant cover that remains in the denuded, exposed channels. So many seasons past have trickled away into vague memory this way, long and unrewarding hours spent in frequently fruitless pursuit of roach in the uninspiring, clear waters of the dying days.

But this is not to say that fish in these circumstances are uncatchable. Every fish has to eat to survive, all the more so when they are driven by hormones prior to the impending spawning season which can be as early as April or as late as early June depending on water temperature and other conditions. Often, roach shoals may be seen cruising and browsing in the river channel when there are clear waters in early March, behaving much as they do in full summer albeit without the security and feeding substrate of thick vegetation. A waggler fished in mid-water with the current, right down the middle of the river, may seem unsubtle and unlikely to produce results, but it can prove an effective means to intercept cruising fish by presenting a bait at eye and mouth level. I have certainly taken roach to 2 lb 11 oz this way when all hope seemed lost, and bigger fish still on the 'lift method' when flows die off almost completely.

But dawn and dusk sessions on remaining areas of better cover have, to me, proved the most rewarding at this time of year. And there are then few better holding features than the perennial and robust protective cover afforded by the submerged roots of bankside alder or willow trees. You don't need to be able to see these fibrous refuges but, due to the thirsty nature of these wetland trees, they will always be there. The roach sometimes crowd into them in dense shoals for their shade, attendant invertebrate food and, above all, refuge from predation. And, when the attentions of cormorants and other piscivores are at their most intense, the roach will pack in all the tighter and closer. Just watch the way a dozen goldfish in a garden pond can crowd under a single lily root or stone when spooked by herons, becoming virtually invisible despite their flamboyant pigmentation. Well, roach are a whole lot better at hiding than that!

I remember one misty dawn at the back end of the season when predation on the river was particularly bad when the neighbouring gravel pits all froze over. Yet I still took a bag of nine 2 lb+ roach from a far bank willow root-ball with only two or three 'back-up' fish, all of which were pushing the magic barrier. Drop the swimfeeder and bread just inches short of the root ball and bites would simply not occur. However, take a risky cast under the tackle-hungry twigs and into the root ball itself and a firm take was all but assured. And this in a two-mile reach of river that had seemed entirely barren of roach all winter, and indeed may well have been throughout much of its length.

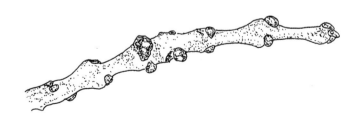

With the exodus of anglers from rivers to stillwaters, and from active to wait-and-bleep angling methods, flowing waters become progressively more neglected with each passing season. This is a blessing to the extent that the river angler has less competition, but a threat when there are less vigilant 'eyes and ears' on the bank and also a reduced economic incentive to protect and manage river fish stocks and the ecosystems that support them. However, some more renowned club waters do see reasonable pressure at popular times, albeit that the crescendo of activity before mid-March and after mid-June is nowhere near what it was before the closed season on stillwaters was lifted. So it was that my attention was caught by one particular popular club water one closing week of the season with the water exceptionally low and as clear as air.

The better-known swims, from which the diligent or fortunate had caught some decent roach, were by this stage well beaten down to bare earth. This sight always sounds alarm bells for me. We anglers know these swims for the pleasure they give us. However, for fish, it is all about survival in the face of potential threats, and so they learn by association far more intensely that certain vibrations, scents, places and a wide range of other subtle sensations besides are to be avoided or actively fled from. As I have written before, beaten-down swim signal beaten-down fish!

My solution is simplicity itself. I look for features, such as submerged tree roots, that lie between the known swims. If fish find a river reach attractive, yet certain 'hotspots' become too hot for them, these features are likely to be the refuges in which they are to be found. With this in mind and by a process of deduction, exploration and laceration by brambles, I found my shoal of big fish one pre-dawn before the world had grown too bright and busy.

Opposite me, a tangle of tree boughs cascaded to touch the river's surface, a dark and safe place of shade and roots beyond them. All I had to do was swing my swimfeeder through a narrow gap between two tackle-grabbing branches. When I say, 'all I had to do', I make rather light of exactly how tight a cast was required, and all the more so given that the far bank was still largely in darkness. Accordingly, my first two casts hit the tangled lattice of twigs, one requiring a new hook and the second a whole new swimfeeder rig. I was relieved not to be sharing the bank with other fisher-folk or dog-walkers that early in the dawn, as my far from mild or kindly self-rebukes may just have raised a few blushes! But this type of precision fishing has its rewards as well as its high stakes, for a bait falling short of cover stands little chance of being picked up.

This is also decidedly one-rod fishing. Normally when legering, I like to fish a pair of quivertip rods not just to cover more lies but because, when two quivertips are positioned close together, it is far easier to discern the attentions of fish from general background disturbances such as the actions of current or breeze. But a single rod also has particular advantages: in this situation, it enabled the quivertip to be scrutinised that much more attentively for often the most minute of bites. Fortunately, this dawn was breaking breathlessly, with current virtually absent, so the backdrop of twigs was perfect as a sight board to help me discern the tiniest telltale nudges of the quivertip. And subtle telltales were all I was expecting, since these roach had been fished for fairly intensively in the past weeks.

On my third cast, the first to penetrate the overhang of twiglets in the half-light, the swimfeeder had barely time to settle before I answered an inquisitive nod on the tip. Sweeping the light leger rod back into that most welcoming of arches, tip held low to the bank top for fear of snaring a branch or flicking the feeder out of the water into its waiting clutches, I felt the buck and plod of a heavy roach. Then, softly and patiently, I kept it from the roots with side strain, allowing it to tire itself out in open water. And, after an uneventful but no less 'heart in the mouth' tussle, a 2 lb 1 oz marvel of silver and scarlet flopped over the waiting rim of my outstretched landing net and was promptly scooped inshore to safety.

What a beautiful way to greet a tranquil March dawn!

I settled the fish gently into my staked pike tube to calm it in the shade of dark fabric and then phoned my fishing buddy to see if he was yet around and wanted in on the party. Fortunately, he was not only up-and-about but also on the bank reasonably close by. By the time he reached me as the dawn light grew stronger, a 2 lb 4 oz roach and another of 1 lb 15 oz had joined the first in the pike tube.

Sensing that we might be into something of a bonanza, but located in a tight 'one-rod-only' swim, my buddy was happy just to sit, chat and enjoy the unfolding action. As light levels gradually increased, accurate casting became a little less of a fraught experience, and we were able to commentate on each successful cast. Right tight to the roots beneath the canopy of branches was clearly where the biggest fish were to be found and so, as each feeder hit the water, we called out the size of fish to expect:

'2 lb 4 oz' … '2 lb 7 oz' … '1 lb 2 oz' … '2 lb 3 oz'.

And with remarkable consistency, these were almost exactly what the Avon scales revealed as my buddy weighed and sacked each fish as I set about catching the next!

The best casts were very much do-or-die, propelled with enough force for the swimfeeder to travel fast and flat under the canopy. But, as the morning light strengthened, I was able to fan the spool rim and abort any more wayward flings and so I happened to land one feeder perfectly into the dark recess, right by the toe of roots. My buddy and I, in jocular unison immediately calling out, '3 lb 1 oz', as the bait plopped into the water.

The quivertip settled and I held my hand nervously over the rod handle, awaiting the most minute of movements. In no more than a minute the quivertip curled round slightly and I slammed into a solid weight, snag or fish? Then the 'snag' kicked back forcefully and I swung the rod tip low downstream to work with the residual flow to draw the fish away from the clutch of submerged roots. This was clearly a very heavy fish, which kited a little before running upstream parallel with the bank. And, when a roach runs and takes line, I always know it is very big and often more than just 'big'.

The fish fought hard, dogged rather than athletic, but I was able to strain it away from any potential snags when it ran too close to them, letting it tire itself out in the clear mid-channel. Soon I was leading it on its side across the still river surface.

Netting and unhooking it, I wrapped it in the waiting damp weight sling and handed it to my buddy, too much on tenterhooks to cast again immediately. He watched the dial scales as he took the strain, waited for them to settle, then spoke just once:

'3 lb 1 oz'!

Whooping with joy, high-fiving, we were giggling like school kids. But then, we suddenly had to conceal the fish quickly in the tube and make ourselves look a little less like cats that had got the cream as another angler sauntered by, asking if we'd had any luck. Of course, we hadn't, except for a couple of small ones, that is!

The fish fed on into full daylight and even as the first shards of sunlight hit the crystal-clear water. Then, as dog-walkers arrived when the dawn gave way to full daytime, it was all over. We totted up the fish. More fish above two pounds than below, including a three-pounder and seven others of more than two pounds. Not a bad near-finale to the season. Wetting a carp sack, I arranged the fish carefully and my buddy took photos before we returned them, thanking each fish as it kicked off strongly back towards its sanctuary under the trees opposite.

This being the 11th of March, we really wondered how to better that in the final couple of days. But, as neither of us wanted to be spotted near a 'hot' swim, we packed up promptly and went our separate ways (breakfast and a shower for me), agreeing to fish different waters together that afternoon and the following couple of days.

These were also notable in their own way, guerrilla fishing in heavily overgrown, neglected swims in a tiny headwater some miles away, often accessed only after some sensitive pruning with secateurs. But the effort was worth it for, over two days, we took several big roach to 2 lb 12 oz.

We returned to the club stretch well before first light on the final day of the season. It was as still and mild as the session just two days before as we set about locating the elusive shoal in the mile or so of river. The fish had not moved far. Once again, I was the lucky boy who stumbled upon them, huddled once again in another set of tree roots beneath a dense canopy of branches.

Now, at this point I should mention that a good angling buddy is a singular breed of creature, and one to which I devote a special entry later on in this book. My buddy was once again happy to watch and share the experience, having already exceeded his self-determined target for the year, including another three-pounder. So, when I called him over having found the shoal in what was definitely another one-rod-only gap between the far bank boughs, he was happy once again to sit and share the experience. I assume it was the same shoal of roach, though none of the fish seemed to be repeat captures judging both by their condition and also subsequent close scrutiny of photographs.

I will not labour the catching, but suffice to say that we repeated our surreal game of guessing the weight of the fish on the basis of the quality of the cast. Sport was brisk, at least when the casts didn't go astray. Indeed, my casting must have been a little better this morning as a spectacular bag of eight fish resulted, including a brace of three-pounders at 3 lb 1 oz and 3 lb 0 oz with backup two-pounders ranging from 2 lb 0z up to 2 lb 14 oz. This was just not normal! Neither was our state of elation. Now, these years later, I can still scarcely believe that the smiling character in the photo with that historical haul of redfins is really me.

As last days of the season go, the river may have looked scarily low, clear and bereft of cover, and the news that others had tried with minimal returns was hardly inspiring. But, somehow, the fish were kind to us, and for some simple reasons beyond the luck of being in the right place at the right time with the right bait and presentation.

Indeed, many valuable lessons emerged from these 'last days' experiences of March 2007, in addition to the valued memories. It shows that, with a little flexibility of thought in your approach, big roach can still be caught when the water is clear and low. Also, that you may succeed where others struggle, simply by doing things just a little differently. In this case, that meant catching reliably a mere 10 yards from known swims that had gone dead. Also that the shoal will be tight into cover and will not emerge, so you'd better be brave and be prepared to lose some kit. Furthermore, that a good angling buddy is something to be treasured, sharing in your successes as you aim to share in theirs, and pooling knowledge to increase the successes of both. In addition, bite detection has to be fine-tuned, for I am sure that other anglers must have had at least some attention from suspicious fish but failed to register this on their set-ups.

The afternoon dusk session on that particular final day were also more than noteworthy, yielding us both more roach including several over 2 lb. And, as dusk settled in the last knockings, my buddy hooked an absolute monster that set his heart racing as he played it nervously out in the dark water before it metamorphosed disappointingly into a 6 lb bream under torchlight in the landing net, and this from a reach of river where no bream had ever been caught or seen before!

But those two dawn sessions over the last few mornings of a dying season, each netting eight roach over 2 lbs including three different specimens over 3 lbs, is something that I will set out to emulate or beat, but never with any expectation of so doing.

And they'll also remind me constantly that great things can occur when you apply yourself differently and diligently despite the circumstances confronting you, a lesson indeed for every aspect of life.

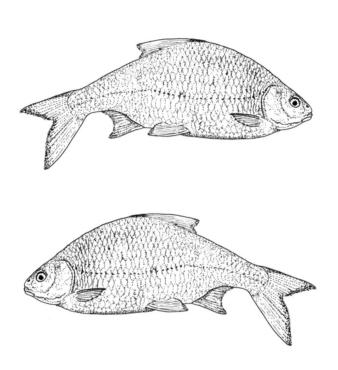

SPRING

CLOSED SEASON MUSINGS

4

Big roach, like this fine brace of 2 lb 5 oz and 2 lb 1 oz taken from the upper
Bristol Avon in March 2009, are things of great beauty

Closed Season Musings

FOR ME, THERE will always be a closed season. This is not just because I am primarily a river angler, where the closed season persists from the Ides of March through to the glorious 16th of June. Rather, it is because I grew up with a closed season.

I still relish the switch to other life priorities when the river season closes, perhaps in part because my birthday falls on the Ides of March. The heart of my fishing year as a river roach enthusiast starts with the New Year and ends with the dying season, during which I pack in as much rod time as I can. My family knows this mania, understands it and forgives me my madness. I save up my leave for time at the 'back end'. The net result is that, whilst this enables me to maximise my chances of river roach at their peak, I also arrive at my birthday feeling pretty jaded and glad that I don't have to get up for a while ahead of increasingly early dawn feeding periods. Yes, I enjoy my closed season on the rivers. And, of course, this makes the dawning of the sixteenth of June all the more glorious.

At the time of the consultation about and then the lifting of the coarse fishing stillwater closed season, I was strongly opposed though realising that the lifting of the closed season was a foregone conclusion almost entirely for commercial reasons. I just felt that the waterside deserved a break. This was not just for the fish, but also whilst birds nested and spring growth flourished. But I could not, and knew I would not, withstand the tide of public and economic wishes.

For the following eleven years, I did not coarse fish at all between mid-March and mid-June though I did cast a fly for game fish and a lure for bass. I spent a lot of time by fresh waters though, both running and still, watching the big fish spawn and also the wider cavalcade of freshwater life. One fine spring morning, for example, I found a very large roach struggling in the margins of the Hampshire Avon with its head caught in a discarded plastic ring used to hold

drink cans together. Cutting that wonderful fish free from the debris of careless humanity, I felt that I had done a good deed and shared a little more of the secret life of roach in quite a different way than when I had arrived with a rod in my hand.

In later years, I started fishing the stillwater 'closed season', though I still do not do so with any great intensity. That said, my personal best roach at the time of writing came from a stillwater at the end of March, a tale yet to be told, as indeed I have had many notable fish throughout all four seasons of the year.

In the spirit of these *Redfin Diaries*, I will therefore relate to you some of these 'closed season' encounters but also a few concluding musings that happen when one is enjoying a break from the headlong pursuit of outstanding roach.

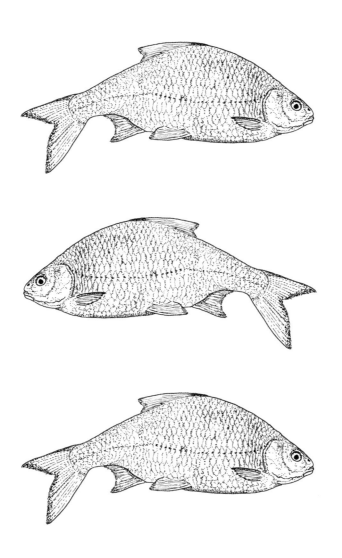

A pristine 2 lb 14 oz roach taken from a flooding Bristol Avon in March 2007

More Than a Feeling

I THINK IT happens to many of us.

I think it happens to many of us many more times than many of us are comfortable to admit.

I think that many of us might feel that the implied element of luck in some way undermines our perhaps over-inflated perception of other skills and sensory acuity.

But sometimes, you just get that feeling.

I can think of many instances of striking on a feeling, and finding myself connected to a big fish for no evident rhyme nor reason.

Though this experience has been repeated too many times to count, one roach in particular comes to mind taken one late winter morning from a river fining down after recent rain. Windless and overcast, this was truly a roach-fisher's dawn, and the sport had been rewarding on Avon float and centrepin. A brace of two-pounders had already graced my net since first light. However, the best of the session had now passed with the growing light intensity.

One option in these circumstances, generally enforced by pressures of work or family life, is to go home, to meetings or otherwise to get on with the other business of the day. Another option is to linger a while longer as, in my experience, the fish often start to move up-river, and to make more use of the cover of river margins than they do during the more confident hours of darkness or half light.

On this fine morning, my angling buddy and I decided to change to a quivertip attack, at least for a short while, casting to the emerging new weed growth in the river margins to intercept any fish that might be cruising there. And this, it turned out, was a sound decision as a few more decent roach made their presence felt by hoovering up our offerings of bread.

However, for neither of us was the day entirely at our disposal, and so my buddy packed up his gear and walked up the bank for a chat as

I made my final casts. Such conversations follow no particular course, veering from observations of fish topping or bubbling, to considering future angling strategies, recollecting successes and failures past, and even straying into some of the frustrations and other matters of the wider world beyond that inhabited by roach. I don't know what we talked about, but I do remember swinging one of my bread-filled swimfeeders down the river tight to the undercut the bank, and launching a second feeder upstream to settle by the roots of an alder tree on the far bank. Both quivertips settled into a gentle bend as the current tightened against the resistance of the terminal tackle, the upstream line describing a slight bow and likely to register as a drop-back bite if a fish paid attention to my bread flake hook bait.

And so we chatted on as the day brightened, signalling a likely end to sport and so time to reel in and go our separate ways. But we must have been talking about something of particular interest, either that or just trying to put off doing other things, because we fished on a while, until suddenly I just got that feeling ...

Don't ask me what triggered it. Both of us had been watching the quivertips intently and had not seen the slightest flicker. But an impulse made me lunge for the quiver rod that had been cast up-current to the alder roots, and to sweep it back downstream into a fighting arc. The light rod bent round and stayed curved as the kick from a strong fish transmitted itself through the cork handle into my right hand, and in a near-automatic movement I knocked off the ratchet on the rear of the reel to let it take line.

Why had I struck? How had I known?

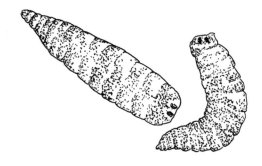

In all walks of life, this phenomenon is repeated: by firemen sensing an imminent building collapse or a blow-back from a fire, by archers just 'letting go' of conscious thought to launch the perfect arrow, by karate or other martial artists who surrender to the same subconscious directions, and of course by anglers too.

Some call it telepathy, others 'feeling the force', intuition, following the flow of Chi, guidance by higher powers, or whatever. For anglers, it is most allied with that marvellous and mystical thing we know as 'watercraft'.

Watercraft may start out as a set of fairly mechanistic deductions, such as recognising 'creases' between fast and slow water as great holding spots for many species of fish, offering protection from currents yet a constant conveyor of food. Then, finding out that at those spots where the leger weight drops just a second longer, or the riverbed ceases to tug on a trotted float, bites are more frequent as one has stumbled on an unseen drop-off. And then you note that certain types of water plants are natural fish-holding spots, or that fish tend to drop into deeper water or head for the shallows as water colour, depth and pace shift. Putting these and many more related experiences together on a new water, you suddenly realise that you are 'reading' swims and that your catch rate increases. The lessons are learned over time, some consciously but many more sinking deeper into the subconscious to form the voodoo that we call 'watercraft'. This progressively helps you developed an instinct about where the fish are, the ideal bait to attract them and the best methods to get it to them.

So too with bite detection. Obviously, some degree of sensory acuity helps. I remember, for example, when I had to meet up with a buddy of mine to discuss publication of one of my books. I was intent on at least casting a line having made the long journey to where he lived and worked. However, time and the fading light were against us, and the river was now just an overhead cast too far away for any meaningful session. Admitting defeat, we opted to drop down to a nearby canal for at least a few cursory casts at the end of a day of bitter air frost. It was, to say the least, hardly auspicious, so my friend opted merely to stand, watch and continue talking about our project whilst

I quivertipped bread against the drop-off of the canal's far bank. Given the unpromising water conditions, I hit a slight tremor on the quiver which, in any other circumstances, would have been dismissed as a zephyr of wind or else a leaf in the current brushing the line. The result was a roach; not a huge one, but a real live one nonetheless on a hugely unfavourable day and piece of water.

After six more roach to maybe half-a-pound and also four or so gudgeon, the darkness and cold finally defeated us. It was time to adjourn to more of our 'formal meeting', and of course a warming cup of tea. As we drove back to my friend's place, he confided that he had not even seen any of the bites.

Super-senses on my part? Hardly, after all, I wear glasses!

ESP? Not likely either.

No, just a half-century of immersion in roach-wrangling that has honed to a fine point the detection of largely subliminal signals, and of trusting my instincts to respond.

Events on that other winter morning on my home river were no different. A hunch, an instinct, a feeling, call it what you may. Something beneath the conscious senses a signal, and something elsewhere in my brain reacts. And so, whether by luck, skill or metaphysics, something distinctly physical was now kicking back against the curve of my quivertip rod. Slowly, the fight came to me, and I raised the rod to keep the fish's head away from the spires of curled yellow water lily leaves that were just now emerging by the near bank riverbed as a precursor to spring.

And, in no time, that wonderful fish lay in the soft folds of my landing net, the two of us anglers gazing down at her broad, scale-perfect flanks as the weak sun finally burned through the morning haze. Such rare sites are to be savoured, all pearl and brilliant red against the fresh green of emerging goose grass. We weighed her at exactly 2 lb 8 oz then slipped her carefully back into the cool river margin, shook hands, and each set off on our separate ways to face the day's commitments.

In all walks of life, there is a temptation to claim credit for subconscious actions that are, in reality, merely unreasoned responses to subconscious signals. And this is why I maintain that all successful angling remains a matter of luck, despite what one's ego or the personality-obsessed media may trick one into believing.

However, one can most certainly hone one's skills and instincts to narrow the odds, and enable one's inner tuition to bring good luck around just that little bit more frequently. In essence, the more you practice, the luckier you get. And the more often you can turn a feeling into something that is more tangible, to cast on a whim to a spot that feels suddenly like it has potential, to change bait or presentation on a hunch, or to hit an unseen bite with confidence, the more successful you'll be.

We've all been there. We all know that this is how it works. And, if we are entirely honest with ourselves, we will all have fluked some pretty decent fish this way to the embarrassment of, or perhaps wilful denial by, our conscious, credit-taking minds.

So the big lesson here is to let go control a little, and hand over to the inner senses. Keep honing the watercraft from which instinct is built, but let your subconscious guide you to more frequent bouts of 'good luck'.

There is no shame in that, to which many a kung fu master would doubtless agree.

A chunky fly-caught roach, GRHE still in its mouth, taken from an early summer Bristol Avon

Fluff

DESPITE MY OBSESSION with hurling bread at often disinterested coarse fish, I am also pretty keen to flick fur and feather about for anything that wants to pay it some attention.

Not that I was born with a silver fly-spoon in my mouth, you understand. Rather, as an ardent reader of Mr Crabtree like so many of us in my early years, I decided that I really should teach myself how to fish the fly despite lacking any opportunity to use the technique in anger. (Not that any fishing should really be conducted literally 'in anger'.)

You see, I lived in lowland Britain, with neither access nor money to get me onto trout rivers and reservoirs, which were then exclusive, expensive and remote. I certainly fished for trout in my later childhood, though this was predominantly in small, heavily-overgrown and almost totally overlooked local streams where it was all one could do to offer a free-lined worm beneath a close canopy of alders, willows and hazels. And lively, colourful and tasty little fish they were too!

So, rather than on the closely-mown banks of hallowed dry fly waters or else afloat on a wind-swept reservoir, my fly fishing experiences started out on a back lawn. This entailed teaming up a small and venerable split-cane fly rod, which I had been handed down by a distant relative at some indeterminate point in time, with a rather decrepit old centrepin reel which I had loaded with string. Largely through bloody-minded persistence, I slowly learnt how to cast a fly without cracking it off and to lay the 'line' gently on the grass. However, rich source though the damp lawn could be for lobworms, fish were conspicuous only by their expected absence.

It was only in much later years that I gathered together the pennies to buy a cheap fly-fishing kit with a real fly line, and to cast it wilfully for real fish. As my experience grew, I came to cast more often for willing coarse fish than for the by then far more widespread and affordable stocked game fish, as I had tired very quickly of farmed rainbow trout. I cast periodically for mackerel too; if you have not yet caught a mackerel from the beach using a light fly rod then you have missed out on one of the planet's most exhilarating, most neglected yet most accessible 'game' fishing experiences.

When I have access to suitable waters, I will gladly fish for wild grayling, brown trout and sea trout today. However, chub, dace and rudd are more frequent targets when I decide to flick the fluff. Predatory fish too are just brilliant quarry, pike in particular putting up a spectacular fight when they sip in a big fly offered in clear winter water.

A great deal of my fly fishing these days also involves travel rods, which I use opportunistically whilst on research and other trips both across the UK and overseas. I have taken mahseer on the fly from Himalayan cascades. A particular fly-fishing favourite are the various yellowfish species of South Africa, which occupy some heavenly places where the mountains sweep down to cradle swift cascades. And of course 'barbel', as the African sharp-toothed catfish is known, which will as eagerly take a fly from the surface as they will underwater, in fact lunging at and engulfing pretty much anything that brushes against their super-sensitive whiskers. I also enjoy my forays for largemouth bass and chub from the Mediterranean rivers of France whilst on family holidays in the summer. All in all, I have had a lot of fun with my light and eminently portable fly fishing gear right around the globe.

Salmon too, or at least that remains an aspiration at the time of writing. You see, I feel I should one day catch a salmon 'properly' on the fly, having hooked plenty over the years, mainly accidentally, on worm and luncheon meat, plug and dead bait. Salmon are also, I have found, extraordinarily partial to swimfeeders, in fact a lot more so than they are to Devon minnows, Tobys and other classic salmon lures. I have also caught many a salmon parr and smolt when waving my carbon fibre wand, but I have yet to latch into an adult grilse or springer on the fly. One day, I still hope.

And of course roach.

Yes, roach.

Roach will eagerly take a fly in the right circumstances. It stands to reason that roach can be tempted to take a fly really, as insect and crustacean life constitute a considerable proportion of their diet during the warmer months. Let's also not forget that roach will also snaffle up small fry with gusto when the mood is upon them. So it should hardly surprise anyone that roach will take an imitation of any of these life forms when presented in the places they may be feeding. This is particularly so in the warmer months. However, the truth of the matter is that roach and chub are both popular targets for fly anglers in the Netherlands all year round, lacking as most of their rivers are in game fish species, and so are probably simply neglected as fly fishing quarry in British waters.

One of the things that I and others have found on my home river, the Bristol Avon, is that the roach have a particular penchant for black flies. No particular pattern, wet or dry, buzzer or pheasant tail, black gnat or black spider, zulu or dark-tied hare's ear, gilt-headed or plain, size 18, 14 or 12. It really doesn't matter all that much, so long as it is black.

Many other folk that I know have also had a lot of success with roach using dark or predominantly black flies, as indeed buff or green patterns, the most successful patterns of which seem to be those that have a generic resemblance to the sorts of submerged insect larvae on which many fish species feed. This ranges from fishing buzzers for roach sipping flies from the surface, to enticing roach to take wet flies ranging from zulus, hare's ears with and without gold ribbing, red tags and pheasant tails. A size 14 hook seems about right and, though I have designed a simply-tied, 'ideal' roach fly (black silk, pheasant tail, peacock herl, silver or copper rib, pheasant cheeks), I will more commonly fall back on the good old GRHE.

As all fly anglers will know, 'GRHE' is shorthand for the gold-ribbed hare's ear, which is available or may be tied in a range of colours from black through greens and buff, and with or without a gold bead head for extra 'flash' and weight. All colours and variants seem to work for, in truth, roach and many other coarse fish are generally fairly non-selective about exactly what it is they are willing to take, unless there is a particularly profuse hatch on the water. (The same is also the case for most game fish.)

There are really only two roach-specific fly fishing tips that I have found. The first of these is to use a weighted fly, be that with a little lead in the tying or else with a bead on the head of the fly. This is because roach are predominantly likely to be feeding in mid-water or near the bottom and also, though they may sometimes be taken in the right circumstances on the dry fly, this way of fishing the sunken fly is more selective when it comes to avoiding rudd, dace and chub. The second tip is to fish close to cover, such as the lee of a reed bed in a river, near submerged vegetation in any conditions, or else beside a drop-off of the bed in still waters. Roach are far more commonly to be found there than in the open water often preferred by trout and rudd.

Not only that, but roach fight really well on fly tackle. I think that this is because a soft fly rod flexes more easily than general coarse rods, allowing a roach to turn away from your pressure as it undertakes its classic bucking motion, and then to run rather than merely to kick side-on. (The same is true of really big roach of three pounds and more, which can more powerfully kick away from the resistance of standard coarse fishing gear and will often then take line in a fight with more 'run' than 'buck', at least until they begin to tire.)

At this point, I have to confess that I've never caught a really big roach on the fly. I've had numerous fish well over a pound but nothing yet over two pounds, though I live in hope. So rather than give you one of my 'Redfin Diary' entries for an encounter with a true monster, I thought I'd reminisce about two days spent with the roach respectively of a certain springtime lake and a summer river.

The lakeside day in question was one of blustery winds, but the water was waking up to the warming rays of late spring. And the idea of fish moving in those warming waters had lured me out too onto the lake bank to see if the roach were responding. The lake itself was in fact rather dull, at least in profile, having been dug at a uniform depth of eight feet with no bars or other features. In fact, the only real features under the water were the deep shoulders of the lake edge, as well as where lanes of winds chopped the surface of the water. Indeed, as I looked out across the expanse of the lake, I could make out the movements of the odd fish, probably rudd, at the interfaces between choppy and still areas of the surface. I knew from experience that a pheasant tail nymph or a hare's-ear, fished at or shortly beneath the surface, would be eagerly sipped in by these golden beauties. However, it was the silver queens beneath, the roach of the mysterious depths, that were on my mind today. And roach I would have.

Sporadic sedges, the occasional olive and a few midges could be discerned battling against the turbulent air, but there was no large or specific hatch of flies. So, favouring a familiar pattern imitative of many types of underwater insect larvae, I tied on a GRHE in the anticipation that the golden bead at its head would carry the fly down below the clutches of those ever-hungry rudd. My plan was to allow the fly to sink sufficiently and then draw it slowly over and along the shoulder of the lake edge to tempt any hungry roach prowling this feature. Takes I had, tentative plucks in the main that didn't quite connect, and I suspected these were from smaller fish, although roach can be remarkably tricky to hook perhaps because they can tend to suck in the fly from the back and not necessarily to have the point of the hook in their mouths. But I did connect with some roach. And then some movement caught my eye in a quiet corner of the lake, down beneath an overhanging sallow.

The movement was that of three mallard ducklings, scooting and darting across the surface under the watchful eye of their mother. The ducklings were, as ducklings do, chasing emerging flies coming off the water. Whilst it is generally true that the predominant diet of a mallard comprises vegetable matter, they are in truth opportunists. And, in their early days, emerging flies can be a really important part of the protein intake of fast-growing ducklings, to the extent that over-stocking with fish in some stillwaters can compromise the ability of these young birds to grow rapidly into healthy adults. There was clearly some kind of a slightly more intense hatch of chironomid midges happening in this quiet arm of the lake, the insects rising from their larval life on the bed to break free into adult flies at the surface. And, if the ducklings and I noticed this, hungry fish certainly would too.

I stalked in closer, far enough away not to disturb the ducklings unduly but sufficiently close to enable me to launch a decent cast into the approximate area in which they were now dabbling and darting. This necessitated a cast almost parallel with the lake bank such that, when I then allowed it to sink sufficiently, my slow and steady retrieve drew the fly along the top of the lake's shoulder.

Bingo! I answered a heavy pluck on the line with a swift raising of the rod, bending into a sprightly fight. This felt different to the rudd I had hit earlier, less of a sidelong rush and more of a steady plod in deeper layers of water. Whilst this roach was of no great size, and the fight was therefore not prolonged, this pretty fish put up a good account of itself. It finally came to my folding net all brilliant silver in the broken sunlight, the red hues of its fins intensified by a warm-water diet rich in insect life.

Roaching on summer rivers can also be huge fun, enabling the inquisitive fishermen to cover miles of bank with the lightest of gear as much to spot fish and watch the wildlife as to actually pursue them with angling intent. But flicking a fly to visible fish can be as immensely enjoyable as it may be rewarding.

I recall in particular one early summer afternoon, again breezy but with intermittent sunshine warming the lazy flow. I had covered perhaps a mile of river, mainly just watching and enjoying what I saw. However, a tight shoal of roach in the lee of a mid-channel bed of round rush caught my attention, and so I set about putting a fly to them to see if they were interested. The cast itself was challenging, 'aerialising' the fly line within the tight confines of bank top willow and alder trees and over a tall stand of nettles behind. This time, I was fishing a green gold-ribbed hare's ear, and I managed to drop it exactly into the slack. Three times, I watched roach peel from the shoal and follow my wet fly as I retrieved it slowly right up to the near bank, before the fish then veered off and back to their haven.

On the fourth cast, I decided to pitch my fly just a little further out, to fall into the fast water near the far bank. Giving it just a moment to sink, I then stripped it back into the stiller water where the roach were milling. And with an impressive thump it was intercepted as it 'swam' into the very lair of the shoal. In the shallow water, I watched the skittering struggle of the roach, dace-like in the rippling sensation transmitted through the carbon blank and cork handle and into my hand, as it sought to run against the pressure of the flexing rod, and feeling quite unlike the staid, bucking fight of a larger roach on standard coarse fishing tackle. She fought well, brilliantly in fact for a roach of a little over a pound in weight, seeking to run yet ultimately spending herself against my giving yet constant resistance. And soon she glinted at the surface, mouthing water as she slid over the rim of my outstretched folding net.

What an early summer jewel! The insect-rich diet of the warming waters had gently gilded her pearlescent flanks, now well mended after the stresses of spawning, her fins outstretched and glowing with the intensity of ripe cherries. The impact with which she had hit the fly, beaded head and fluffy green body visible in her mouth, had signalled the intensity of her hunger.

After a lingering look and a quick photograph, I held her momentarily in the warm river margins before she kicked off strongly, finding once again the cover and kin from whence she had so recently been drawn.

I would be lying to say that fly fishing is one of my favoured, 'go to' methods of roach fishing. However, in these perfect moments, as indeed when I really fancy coarse fishing but have only access to trout waters, it is indeed a perfect way to entice such brilliant jewels from clear, warm waters.

It is an unexplored yet readily-accessible pleasure that, I suspect, still awaits discovery by many an admirer of that most beautiful of fishes, the roach.

A bright 2 lb 11 oz comes to net from a swollen Bristol Avon in January 2007

Roach Angling Partners

WHATEVER A TROTH is, most of us at one time or another in our lives pledge it to a significant other (or in many cases more than one 'significant other'). Yet life is a far more complex thing than that assumed by our narrow cultural conception of 'a meaningful relationship'.

With our big brains, our capacity for language and non-verbal expression, and our capabilities of synthesising disparate ideas into new concepts, we are above all *Homo interactus*: evolving organisms seemingly designed to build complex relationships. We do so, or at least have the ability so to do, both with the environment that supports us and with those with whom we share it.

We also build relationships across space and time, compelled by our nature to innovate writing and other information technology to share intelligence beyond our narrow geographical range and life spans. The ancient Greeks speak to us fluently today in their surviving writings, but more profoundly so in the way that their and others' revelations and accrued knowledge have shaped our inherited conceptions and assumptions of justice, science, philosophy, divinity and so many other warps of the fabric of contemporary culture.

Throughout the 100,000 years of human history we've inherited languages, forms of music, painting, agriculture, dance, architecture, civil and religious ceremony and other societal traditions, all of them embodying rich veins of expression and meaning assimilated like the fine grains that comprise the wood of a tree. To these, we add the weft of our own discoveries and inventions, environmental understanding, computing and machine intelligence, psychology, new music, novel literature, film and so many other things besides, to build a new, ideally even more evolved tapestry.

This is the magic carpet upon which we ride throughout the brief span of our incarnations. And as we do so we weave into it our own unique filaments, handing these on as a legacy to our direct descendants and others yet unborn around this beautiful planet, and to lives and worlds that are yet to be.

Relationships then are the stuff of humanity, be that life partner, children, broader family, work colleagues, voluntary associations, pub and other local communities, or … fishing buddies. Each can be as complex and profound as the next, and not in any competitive sense. Each is just a different facet of our complex human natures.

I am, or at least have been, a solitary angler by nature for much of my life. For me, understanding the fish is central. Struggling to comprehend, or more commonly failing to comprehend, the mystery of how fish are behaving, and how, where and on what they may be feeding, is a detective adventure that would surely intrigue even Conan Doyle. Then seeking, however ineptly, to outwit them with my clumsy tactics adds further layers of challenge again.

Whereabouts are these fish? Where are they within the water body, and which particular different habitat, water depth and cover are they making use of as conditions change by the season or the minute? What food are they taking and when, or what may I best wean them on to instead? All this research is painstaking and exhausts a great deal of the time available between family, work, charitable, social and sleep needs. So, free though I am with my general approach and the lessons I have learnt, I am not about to tell the whole world exactly where I have tracked down my elusive fish!

Nevertheless, I acknowledge that I stand on the shoulders of giants (and some pygmies too). The angling greats have spoken eloquently to me through their writings. Walker, Venables, Walton, Stone, Sheringham and so many others have forged rules, both written and unwritten, that shape our implicit perceptions and broad specimen approach. Other greats still living have been friends, though I have also known quite a few who think themselves great but who have in reality contributed very little and instead merely surfed waves generated by others. But the key principle remains. None of what I do have I done alone, even though I might do it alone.

And yet, every now and again, a significant angling other has become a key part of my piscatorial life. Parallel to the 'no (or at least tolerably few) secrets' instinct that seems to arrive unbidden in a loving relationship, every now and again one finds oneself sharing freely with someone who's angling instincts and values coincide. Just as a growing love affair can be nourished by the synchronicity of finding oneself repeatedly in the same place and time as another, so too one may find that the potential perfect angling buddy arrives unannounced but often at the same swim or water that one has selected. Akin to the way in which nascent intimacy is cemented by the often unguarded sharing of secrets and beliefs held dear, so too the emerging angling relationship flourishes because the defences drop involuntarily to share secrets of swims, timings, effective innovations and cunning baits.

Like all relationships, two minds and souls can then combine to innovate beyond the capacities of each alone. Like all effective relationships from any walk of life, from sport to science, unexpected results become possible. And, before one has really become conscious of it, an evolving angling partnership has been born with each applauding and encouraging the successes of the other.

I have enjoyed very few such enduring angling partnerships throughout my long angling life, but all have been fruitful beyond any reasonable expectation. All take one to places, both physical and conceptual, beyond comfort zones. All make one more complete and leave a residue of changed perceptions and values. All have challenged established beliefs. This capacity for suspending fixed assumptions, however successful to date, to make space for new innovation, discovery and fresh approaches, is a hallmark of such a functional relationship.

But, like any human relationship, there are ups and downs. In scientific research, for example, there will be lean periods of metaphorical (and literal) wearing out of shoe leather and washing of test tubes, though all the while knowing that the very next step could lead to a fresh and inspiring discovery that could propel one in new directions. So too in business relationships, where it would be wholly unrealistic for each step to result in a breakthrough. Most, as we know well, will merely be to steady the ship or 'tick the boxes' of the management system. So it goes in all levels of government, where the 'meat-and-two-veg' of interactions is about maintaining social fabric rather than instigating progressive policy. Also in family life, the exercise of the law, and so in fishing partnerships.

Sometimes, it is enough just to hang out, to share lifts to venues, to drink whisky and tell tall angling tales, or merely to challenge one's angling buddy's safer assumptions. Like any relationship, its intensity will wax and wane. Oftentimes, simple collective enjoyment is enough, or even plodding along together during those inevitable times of friction, knowing that all people, oneself included, have the capacity to be irritating from time to time! But the next cast or flash of inspiration could lead to a new phase of unforeseen excitement and angling success. One works and aspires for that next moment to come alive.

Like any relationship, one also has to allow space. The security of the relationship should form a seed crystal around which others can revolve in the trust that inner values are safe between the principal players. Shared secrets must always be respected and guarded as one finds different types of interaction with other people.

One might have a dalliance with another friend on a new or foreign water, sparking off one another to generate fresh ideas, approaches and successes beyond the expectation of each individual. One such dalliance led to my personal best roach taken from a Northern Ireland stillwater about which I have yet to tell you. Another led to my first Indian mahseer trip and a string of other fish caught by methods that no one before had thought to use, but which me and another mate bounced around between us as an amalgam of ideas born of his match technique, my specimen experience and our collective observations by the waterside.

However, then one comes home. All such productive relationships can coexist, at least in the absence of competition or suspicion. Openness and mutual support are the underpinnings of any strong relationship in any walk of life, personal, working or playing, relationships that grow through evolving interactions that further each party's angling enjoyment and success.

So what are the knacks of finding such a perfect angling partner? The first is to realise that there is no such thing as a perfect partner in any walk of life. We are all unique, and as such we will delight and frustrate others in equal measure as, in their turn, they will do so to us. Know this, accept this, and the good bits will become evident as one learns that any valued relationship is more about controlling one's own idiocies than it is about seeking or expecting perfection in another.

Another vital realisation is that the ideal angling buddy is not sought, for example through websites, cards in the newsagent's window, angling dating agencies or other means, either literal or metaphorical. Rather, such potential partners find each other.

One has plenty of offers to form such a partnership when one's face is known in the 'big fish' angling press, but this is by and large not from the type of common core value systems from which an enduring and functional relationship can grow. This then leads to another important principle: that of letting it grow naturally. Relax, focus on your own angling approach, and just let it happen, or not, as it is destined so to do.

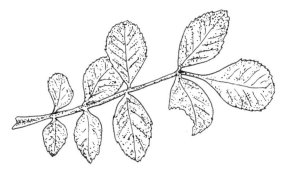

Bread flake presented with quivertip and cage feeder can be devastatingly effective for big winter roach, but modification of tactics can be helpful to stay ahead of the game

The Tackle Tinkering Arms Race

SOMETIMES, ONE STUMBLES across a method that just works. This may be through patient innovation, a matter of chance, or by a process of 'monkey see, monkey do'.

Of the latter, I will tell you of a brace of 2 lb 7 oz roach taken from a short stretch of water from which it had got increasingly hard to entice roach, any roach, as flows declined and colour dropped from the water. My buddy and I flogged away with float and quiver, for good roach were certainly present, progressively fining down our tactics and hook lengths with ever-smaller baits and hooks to match. Our successes were far from proportionate to our persistence. And then, one afternoon, another angler with considerably less experience dropped into a swim immediately above a near-bank alder that had been kind to us previously, casting in stale bread on a big hook to 6 lb line. He proceeded to haul out quite a few roach, including one of about 2 lb 3 oz

I dislike the disparaging term 'noddy', often used by the self-defined specimen elite in a derogatory way to describe perceived lesser anglers, and I dislike it for a number of reasons. Firstly, there is room on this Earth for all sorts of people, including those who are content just to sit and fish without making a big issue of it. Secondly, those who do make a big issue of it should not mistake this as a mark of superiority over others. Thirdly, to dismiss any successful tactic is to blind yourself to learning, and it is my belief that none of us are so perfect or superior in any walk of life that we should be averse to learning from whatever source. Those blind to learning or respect are the real 'noddies'.

I can tell you without embarrassment that, the very next afternoon, I was back at that alder-hung swim with a quivertip rod and link-leger presented on 6 lb line. What's more, I caught well, including the two 2 lb 7 oz roach that I've just mentioned!

189

'Monkey see, monkey do?' Well, sort of, but also with a little bit of 'monkey think' thrown in for good measure. Late season roach that have seen considerable angling pressure grow wary, and particularly so as the water clears. Thus, alerted to the attentions of anglers, not to mention other predators to which they are highly vulnerable in low and clear water, they will very often cram themselves in tight shoals into any available cover. Though frequently invisible from the bank top, balls of underwater roots beneath bankside willow or alder trees are particularly attractive. As I said before, cast a few inches short of them, and the roach are unlikely to venture out, at least in daylight. But hit the 'sweet spot' tight to the roots, and a sweet time may just be had.

And so, I figured, a light line and cage feeder would settle inches too far out from the security of those near-bank alder roots despite even the most risky or lucky cast under the tackle-grabbing awning of its branches. But cast in using 6 lb line, and the pressure of water on the thicker filament would roll the light link-leger right into the taking zone. And so it proved that day, and many other days besides. Cast, settle, roll, settle again, thump! A fine bag of roach too, with some *bona fide* specimens when excessive subtlety could not place the bait where the fish wanted it. A consistent message is emerging here ...

As the fish I pursue learn, a perpetual 'arms race' has ensued, resulting in me modifying my float and ledger rigs over the past decades, tweaking and experimenting, almost as often failing, but every now and again moving my approach forwards and sometimes in counter-intuitive ways. I have already mentioned, as an example that need not be repeated here, how my waggler attack on wind-swept rivers can involve a big and seriously under-shotted waggler float such that the large amount of quill sticking out of the water ('noddy' fashion) lets me work my bait across and thereby read the riverbed. It's not quite gossamer match tactics, but it has proved perfectly adequate for 3 lb+ roach and many two-pounders in the right circumstances!

And then there is the masonry nail. Though I say so myself, my use of masonry nails in heavy trotting is nearly legendary, at least to the extent that many who know of my trotting approach and its red-finned and other triumphs down the years may also have heard of my keen use of masonry nails. Let me tell you the story of how I came to use them, and why I have stuck with them for a quarter-century.

Trotting a big float from a centrepin reel on a long rod is a supremely enjoyable and enormously successful way of winkling out roach when winter rivers are flowing strongly. This is because they enable an angler to search out fish along the riverbed, and also to read the features of the water as the float swims downstream. However, a heavy float is essential. By heavy, I count a two-and-a-half swan shot float as a *de minimus*, a four or five swan shot float as common, and I will use floats larger still when flows are harder or the water is deeper. I recall one day back in the late 1980s on the Hampshire Avon when I was fluttering sprats for pike to 17 lb one Sunday morning under a four-swan float then, after lunch, turned my attentions to roach to 2 lb 4 oz in the afternoon trotting bread under a heavier five-swan float! As they say, horses for courses.

The reason for using such bulky floats is down to the phenomenon of laminar flow. This is the phenomenon of water moving at different speeds in a channel, the faster water flowing at the surface of the river where resistance is slightest but becoming progressively slower near the bed and banks where there is the greatest friction, sometimes creating slack zones near significant obstructions. It is due to laminar flow that you may often see a trout or salmon holding station in torrential flows, with barely the exertion of the occasional flicker of the fins.

The fish has found a lie where the resistance of a boulder, log or drop-off in the streambed creates a cushion of near-static water. Likewise, in the healthy flows of a clear chalk river, one may occasionally spot a big fish or a shoal of them facing downstream. This occurs when a gyre (vortex) in the riverbed, generally caused by a depression or obstruction, causes the flow of water to fold back on itself.

The same phenomenon of the loafing trout or the 'backwards fish' applies to one degree or another in all flowing waters. The rapid pace of unimpeded water at the surface can belie slacker currents at increasing depths, particularly on the riverbed where resistance is greatest. And so, in strong river flows, one has to have a float bulky enough to hold back hard against the surface current to enable the bait to 'walk' at the languid pace of the waters at the riverbed. Ideally, one should aim to inch the float through the swim by exerting gentle thumb pressure on the drum of a centrepin reel, as it is in these slacker flows that roach will most likely be found avoiding excessive exertion but making use of food washed down to them.

Of course, holding back the float is no good unless there is some sort of bulk weight on the line beneath it to carry the bait down to where the fish are swimming. Otherwise, the bait would simply be flailing around in the current behind the float. Then, a 'dropper shot' between the bulk shot and the hook is necessary to bring the bait itself in touch with the riverbed or other chosen feeding depth. A lighter float and counterbalancing shot may seem 'sensitive', but I'm afraid that the bait will at best waft around ineffectually above the riverbed or else be ripped along in an unnaturally rapid or erratic manner.

Like many, I used to use a 'pearl necklace' of split shot as bulk weight. But then I started to experiment.

A string of shot may be readily affixed to the line but there are, to my mind, far too many downsides. A split shot can weaken the line as it is pinched onto it, and a series of shot can create a chain of weak links. Then the shot can flex against each other as the line bends, particularly on casting and retrieving, stressing or gnawing away at the weak spots. The hook link can fold back and snare on the line of shot, fouling the baited hook. And, of course, all of these problems are exacerbated by anything beyond the shortest and gentlest of casts.

By the late 1980s, when tube shot came on the market, I thought I'd found a great replacement. Tube shot constitute a tube of heavy metallised rubber cut (or broken) to the required length and weight, and through which the main line is then threaded. Though it did the trick for me, tube shot proved far from perfect. In the hostile hot-cold, wet-dry environment of a tackle box, the metallic rubber tended to 'weep' out some of its plasticiser content, coating other bits of tackle in sticky oil and also making the tube shot brittle with age. Then the stopper shot used to prevent the tube from running the whole way down the line occasionally trapped the hook length on longer casts. But tube shot were nonetheless a step forwards, and many and large roach came my way as a consequence.

Then there were supply problems. Suddenly, I could not find any tube shot. So should I go back to split shot, or should I innovate? Taking the latter path, I experimented with various bulk weights including driller leger weights (good for pike floats but generally far too heavy for trotting), sections cut from coat hanger wire (rusted away too quickly) or welding rods (too variable in properties), pole float olivettes (too expensive) and all manner of other bizarre bulky weight variants.

What I needed was something manufactured cheaply, of a heavy and non-corrosive material, and of consistent weight. And one day, doing some DIY around the house, I found the solution literally in my hands. Spraying up three sizes of masonry nails firstly with metal primer and then with black paint, I instantly had bulk shot matched to my three main sizes of float that could be attached to the line top-and-bottom with rig tube. Eliminating shot and easily moved or swapped for a different sized weight without line damage, I have never looked back after first using these masonry nail bulk shot, even when tube shot came back on the market. I heartily recommend the humble, cheap and abundant masonry nail to anyone who is interested, and I even use them as interchangeable leger weights by plugging them into float adapters.

I now also use swivels of different weights in place of a dropper shot, eliminating split shot entirely from my rig and also dealing with excessive line twist as the tackle is retrieved. I've messed around with reel line and hooklengths of different diameters, colours and buoyancies, as well as hooks of various patterns and wire diameters. Also, I don't use traditional Avon floats often now, favouring at first loafer patterns and then Bolognese-style floats to ride the water better, show me more tip to spot at distance and in choppy waters, and to 'cut' back on the strike without too much surface disturbance. But the masonry nail remains, and shows no signs of being upgraded in my tackle box in the next quarter century.

My leger rigs have also become a focal point in the 'arms race' with increasingly suspicious roach, grown hypersensitive to the slightest resistance. Like most of us, I suspect, I started off legering with a general-purpose float rod, passing the line through the eye of a proprietary bomb or feeder, and then feeling for bites or else watching the rod tip for movement. Then I used a screw-in quivertip to enhance sensitivity to movements, graduating later to dedicated quivertip rods. As time passed, it troubled me that the eyes of my leger end-tackle easily became snarled in weed, algae or the soft mud of some stream or pool beds. And so I tied on booms of a few inches of stiff 14-17 lb nylon to stand them off a short way, using a swivel to connect to the reel line to combine the virtues of paternoster and leger rigs in the reduction of resistance to taking fish. And my catch rate increased, and life was good. However, it bothered me that I was not connecting with all of the more subtle pulls of wary fish, and perhaps was not even seeing those of roach that had grown warier still.

The next modification was to combine the boom approach with the match angler's loop method, retaining the swivel in a loop of reel line and tying off the far end with a series of three double-overhand water knots to create a slightly stiffer boom to help prevent the hook link, connected loop-to-loop, from snagging with the bomb or swimfeeder. By eliminating the impediment of a split shot, swivel or leger stop beneath the point of attachment of the weight, bites were more confident and also hit rather more reliably. But missing some bites still bugged me.

Long before, I had messed with the quivertips themselves to optimise bite detection. Heating the tip ring with a flame, I melted the glue and removed the ring then placed a silicone float adapter onto the tip before gluing the ring back. Plugging a betalight into the float adapter, I was able not only to spot bites into dusk and darkness but also to have a better end-point to help me spot shy bites by day. Also, I sourced the softest tips I could find to ensure that the slightest take could develop into a confident pull with less risk of resistance betraying me, and I also learnt to hit the slightest suspicion of movement which often betrayed the biggest and most cautious fish.

The 'business end' of the tackle still bothered me, and so I modified my ever-evolving rigs still further by masking knots in the boom between swivel and bomb/feeder using rig tubing. Not content with the visibility and bulk of that, I later invested in green, brown and black shrink-tube to streamline and camouflage still further the knots either end of the boom.

Subsequently, I replaced the 14-17 lb monofilament boom with a loop of 4 lb line tied to the feeder, the swivel running free within that loop, to eliminate even the rigidity of the stiff nylon. My catch rates increased while successive hard winters made the roach fishing increasingly difficult. I know that I will not stop tinkering, but the default leger rig that I have arrived at to date is as follows:

- Soft, paired fibreglass quivertip rods, for their more forgiving through action than modern carbon fibre blanks.
- The softest 'donkey tips' that I can find to insert into the rods to refine bite detection, each modified by the addition of a float adapter and betalight.
- Micro swimfeeders or bombs (often masonry nails plugged into float adapters) connected by a loop of four-pound nylon to a swivel.

- Size 12 fine-wired spade-end hooks for bread flake so that the bulk and weight of metal is minimised.
- A wide rod rest head on which to position the quivertip for optimal visibility.

Like my waggler, trotting and other rigs, my legering approach will continue to evolve according to my observations, deductions and personal quirks, as part of an ongoing 'arms race' with fish, the sensitivity of which I grow increasingly to appreciate.

But I use the metaphor of the 'arms race' in the most gentle way possible, as fish can never be my opponents. Rather, the fish that I pursue are my inspiration and tutors, which I hold in the highest regard for their amazing and sometimes infuriating wariness.

Do my rigs help? And, if so, why? Well, I believe they eke out a little more luck for me, and my fishing diary bears that out to a fair degree. But whether this is because they impart greater confidence to the fish is a moot point. It may be that they merely impart greater confidence to me, for an enhanced belief that catching big roach by design on a consistent basis is possible can, of itself, make it possible.

Or maybe all this tinkering just keeps me thinking about the roach and how they are going about the precarious task of surviving, and so merely tunes me in a little better to their changing habits?

Perhaps I'll never know why what works does work. Indeed, perhaps it will never matter why it works, just so long as it does.

My life has in many ways been defined by this 'arms race' with cold-blooded, small-brained creatures, which nevertheless continue to outwit me most of the time! But, if this makes me an angler that succeeds a little more but enjoys and respects river life a lot more, I'm happy to be so defined.

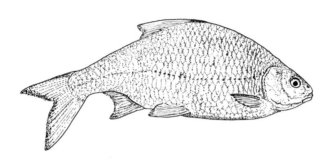

Six 2 lb+ roach (the biggest 2 lb 6 oz) and one of 1 lb 14 oz taken from a strongly flowing Bristol Avon on a dawn session in March 2009

Make Hay while the Sun Shines

AS I SEEM to keep reiterating, my apparently unprecedented success with roach is all down to luck. Sure, the scientific thinking I bring to bear on finding and tempting fish tends to make me luckier than most. But let's not flatter ourselves about the major factor at play here. To think otherwise is to deceive others and to put unbearable pressure on oneself.

Clever thinking can put you in the right place at the right time, with the right bait presented in the right way. But there clearly needs to be fish there to catch. And in that regard, I have really fluked my way to success on quite a number of occasions.

Considering roach angling in summer, I mention that I lucked into a particularly rich year class of chunky specimens in a largely overlooked estate lake at just the time when commitments outside of education were few. It was then a matter of working out how to present tempting baits to them where and when they were hungry. And then, considering successes in autumns gone by, I told the tale of stumbling upon the 'roach pond' in a secluded woodland edge where a small head of specimen roach were to be found in places that their smaller peers dare not venture due to the proliferation of hungry perch.

I was equally lucky in the timing of my move to the banks of the Hampshire Avon in the mid-1980s. By that time, the true glory days of the river may have been well behind it. Having first fished the Hampshire Avon in 1965, I can tell you that tales of golden gravels and shoals of salmon parr voracious for pretty much any small bait are no mere figment of rose-tinted nostalgia. The river really was that profuse and beautiful!

The Hampshire Avon twenty and more years later was a rather different beast. Thirty and forty years further on, the pressures upon it are even more intense and diverse, and the fishing incrementally harder.

The fish fauna of the Hampshire Avon has mirrored the changing fortunes and character of the river. A trustworthy older friend who fished the river in the 1960s in a rather more grown-up way than my then childish dabblings tells me of catching a trio of two-pounders in a lunch-hour break during a working day. This was far from the norm, to be sure, but serves as an indicator of sorts of the decline of the river by the time of my relocation to its banks in the late 1980s. However, my own later magic window too was a bit of a special era, with some strong year-classes of roach coming through and, happily for me, when my work-life balance was rather better poised than it is today. (Mismanagement of the life-fishing balance during my thirties, and its wider social ramifications, is another matter entirely!) The net result was a period of marvellous fishing, lots of big roach and a growing media profile as I made the transition into journeyman hunter of specimen fish of many species.

However, as my friend John Bailey and I often reflect of our respective experiences of Norfolk's River Wensum and the Hampshire Avon, we had not then realised the chronic sickness of the rivers that we loved. A healthy river produces many fry from abundant and suitable spawning and nursery areas, where good water quality, habitat, plant and invertebrate communities nurture their survival and growth, predation is balanced, and flows are sustained. Our respective chalk rivers were much afflicted across all of these parameters, further challenged by alien invasive species of vegetation and animals as well as diverse and increasingly exotic pollutants from towns, roads, industry and intensifying farming. The net result was a strangulation of the fish fauna and the wider ecosystem, hacking away at its vitality from its very roots. Declining flows, siltation of gravels and the loss of native vegetation and habitat has a devastating impact on the successful recruitment of juvenile fish into the population. Often, the most obvious first symptom may seem like a good thing, the proliferation of larger fishes which pack on weight in the absence of competition for food from the normally far greater numbers of their smaller peers. Our respective 'golden eras' were, with hindsight, early spasms in the decline of rivers now compromised in their capacity to regenerate fish stocks.

Few big roach are found throughout the Hampshire Avon today, except perhaps at Britford where clever and dedicated management of the river and its connected former water meadows and wetlands is safeguarding stocks and their regeneration. (Ironically, poor management of Britford in the 1980s had meant that it had less good roach whilst much of the rest of the river prospered.) I was just lucky to relocate to the Hampshire Avon when a strong head of big roach was there for the taking, as indeed I am fortunate today to have good friends at Britford.

A change of job and life circumstances saw me relocate in the early 1990s to the Bristol Avon, a river with little specimen profile and one into which I had never before cast a line. A new challenge and a new phase of life. What was I to expect? Well, certainly not what I found. As I narrated when considering autumn roach, my exploration of this new river was a pleasure and a surprise. And after banking my first Bristol Avon 'two' on my first February on the river, it was as if a specimen roach tap turned on for me. And it didn't stop gushing until the 'perfect storm' of troubles of the two crippling winters of 2009–10 and 2010–11 wiped out a huge mass of roach stocks, right across the year classes.

I think that I can claim that my scientific, flexible and persistent approach was a contributory factor to my often dramatic successes. (A multi-year survey by *Angler's Mail* of the specimen potential of British counties revealed that nearly 90% of Wiltshire's specimen fish reported in the preceding few years were mine.) However, the two separate 'golden eras' throughout my first twenty years of getting to know the Bristol Avon (the severe winter of 1996–97 was also a major

A personal best roach of 3 lb 11 oz taken on my first night with Keith Berry on his 'record roach lake' in Northern Ireland

Whoppers from the Record Roach Lake

THE BRITISH RECORD (rod caught) roach at the time of writing is Keith Berry's marvellous 4 lb 4 oz fish taken from a Northern Irish lake at the end of March 2006. Keith tells us all about it in his Foreword to this book.

Keith is a skilled and patient tench specialist, but also an all-round coarse specimen angler who had been pike fishing at this lake early in that winter. What he saw priming in the lake margin fairly made his eyes pop from his head, albeit that the fish he saw seemed too big to be roach. But the images of those fish kept returning. So, in March, he returned with scaled-down leger tackle, complete with paternostered maggots and a swimfeeder presented with a swingtip for optimal sensitivity. Keith targeted the big roach that he had seen very much by design, adapting his technique and using every ounce of his experience to eventually bank his famous fish.

In this regard, Keith had much in common with the late Bill Penney, holder of the long-running 3 lb 14 oz record roach taken from Walthamstow Reservoir in 1938. Whilst Bill was a roach specialist, and indeed had long experience and a track record of specimen fish from that reservoir, both anglers were targeting outstandingly large roach very much by design and with a great deal of skill.

Scanning the record books, the same cannot be said of many other former holders of the roach record. This is not a problem as a record fish confers neither fortune nor endorsement of superior skill upon its captor (though I have certainly dealt with previous record-holders who believe that this is so and who behave abominably to others). Indeed, there is something comforting about the fact that many former records have fallen to lucky folk with no particular talent.

Keith, however, was very much targeting what was to be the record fish, and which he was also to catch once again the following week at the slightly lighter weight of 4 lb 3 oz. He went on to catch many more

3 lb+ roach over the following couple of years, including a different fish at the record-equalling weight of 4 lb 4 oz.

When Keith Berry and I shook hands for the first time, we were certainly no strangers. I had first encountered him the year before, shortly after I had been asked to identify his 4 lb 4 oz record claim. I was happy to confirm it unambiguously as a true roach. Once the bureaucracy was out of the way, I contacted Keith. A friendship ensued from that first call to congratulate him, and to ask for a quote and permission to use his photo as my tome *The Complete Book of the Roach* neared publication. We phoned each other often thereafter to discuss matters piscatorial, and our families exchanged cards. But I never expected the most precious of all invitations.

So here I was, camped out on the shore of 'that secret lake' in Northern Ireland. What a treat. Circled by Norfolk reed, willow scrub and fields, the peat-tinged water exuded both mystery and promise. And, as the breeze fell away after we had set up our tackle and shelters, some eye-poppingly vast roach began to prime ...

Keith was as keen to see my approach as I was to learn his. Our methods reflected our respective specialities. Keith's primary passion is for tench and so he opted for a swimfeeder and maggot attack with the swingtip, tightened up at night to electronic alarms. I am primarily a river angler and so that shapes my thinking. Immediately prior to my Northern Ireland trip, I had experimented with helicopter, bolt and all manner of other rigs besides before eventually settling on a method not a million miles different to my standard ultra light river quivertip tactics, these too tightened over electronic alarms at night.

I have a mixed history with this type of static, self-hooking approach. Back in the late 1980s, I vowed never to have anything to do with this new-fangled static 'buzzer/bolt-rig/bivvie/boilie' style of fishing that had sprung up during my few years away from regular angling following university and an early research career. Why would I want to sleep when fishing? So, when I started once again to night fish for pike, zander, eels, tench and large perch, I would often sit awake half the night, fighting sleep and hypothermia as I hunched, under an onslaught of dew and frost, staring at bobbins suspended in torchlight. Oh, I missed bites aplenty! And, the following days, I was almost completely non-functional too. And then I started fishing a new water for tench that, one day we just knew, would smash the ten-pound barrier (which was almost unheard of in the late 1980s), but where a bite per twenty-four hours was about normal. And so I bought a buzzer … then an overwrap for my brolly … then I relented on the use of boilies though insisted on ones with 'natural' flavours (mainly seed-based at the time) … and finally kitted up with a bolt rig and bought a bed-chair! Today, I will use this kit when conditions necessitate, though I will meticulously avoid it when they don't.

And so we arrived at that most tantalising of lakes (me with some spare camping kit borrowed from Keith to save on excess baggage fees on the flight across the Irish Sea) and set up our rods up over buzzers for the long night ahead.

That first evening, Keith and I talked incessantly, telling tales and supping on a good many cans of beer as the light faded. Then, as if to welcome or perhaps to taunt us, some awesome roach top-and-tailed perhaps four or five rod-lengths out.

It intrigued me why the roach were topping in twenty-plus feet of water. Members of the carp family do so to adjust buoyancy, lacking gas glands and so needing to gulp air manually into their swim bladders. So where were these fish going to feed if they needed increased buoyancy? They would surely not be feeding in open water where the food was sparse or, more likely, absent in these cold waters. Making a number of exploratory casts with my swimfeeder, counting down its descent, I found a narrow shelf where the steep edge of the lake levelled out briefly at about twelve feet. I promptly deposited one of my rigs, baited with red maggots, onto this interesting feature. The second swimfeeder was cast into the deeper water, where the steep edge levelled off again at a depth of twenty-two feet.

207

On both rods, I had impaled one rubber maggot and two live ones on the hook to provide neutral buoyancy so that the bait would waft naturally up from the lake bed when disturbed by the pectoral fins of passing fish.

However, the fish were not yet ready to disturb our peace. Our maggot baits lay untroubled, save for a couple of line bites to Keith's rods. So the speculations, anecdotes, bacon butties and beer flowed into darkness. We retired early under a full moon, with the promise of four nights ahead of us.

With the stillness of the night, I set my bobbins on a long drop behind the alarms in the hope of reacting quickly to any subtle indications. However, neither bites nor sleep came easily as the temperature crashed to -4°C. Despite this, we were both loathe to close our respected bivvie and tent doors in case of missing a blip on the indicators.

Then, suddenly, I was wrenched from my dosing at half-ten by the shriek of my right-hand indicator. A heavy fish had picked up the red maggots I'd offered on the twelve-foot ledge, and it was taking line against the reel's loosened drag. I stumbled out in my socks into the darkness and the icy, wet mud, too eager to bother with such trivia as wellies! Bending into a powerful fish, I tightened the drag and knocked off the anti-reverse as the fish powered, tench-like, first to my left then to my right. Too muscular to be a roach, surely? But soon the fight was coming to me, as the fish rolled through the dead reeds in the margin.

I picked up the landing net, feeling the layer of ice under my hand, and brought the fish over it. Only then could I fumble in my pocket for a torch and look down at a jaw-dropping vision of silver and scarlet that totally filled the net head.

Keith, by this stage, had stirred from slumber and called out to see if I was into a fish. I'd better not repeat my reply exactly; it was along the lines of: 'Well Crikey, it's jolly well a jolly big roach!' In truth, for all my education and supposedly literary capabilities, I couldn't think of a single word that didn't begin with 'F'.

We both gazed in amazement at the fish under lamp-light, too big to be real, before turning the unhooking mat over to get rid of the layer of ice. Keith zeroed the scales whilst I removed the hook, and then the moment of truth ... 3 lb 11 oz!! A new PB by nearly five ounces. Keith also pointed out that it was 11 oz above the official Irish record. (He should know, having at that time already taken six Irish roach above 3 lb including his two 4 lb+ fish.)

We stashed the roach carefully in a pike tube, pegged at both ends, the kindest way of keeping a large and delicate specimen like this, then chatted over a celebratory beer for maybe half-an-hour whilst the adrenaline subsided.

The night passed unsettled. I was getting frequent line bites, and every time I left the relative comfort of the ice-crusted tent I grew colder and colder. I was not made of the same stuff as these hardened Irish specimen anglers and my flimsy tent and underpowered thermal clothing most certainly weren't either. Each time, I cast shorter and shorter. I was even getting line bites in two feet of water under the rod tip! The roach, it seemed, were priming to exploit food on the shallower edges of the lake under the cover of darkness. However, no real take materialised.

By dawn's cold light, I was totally knackered, and the sleeping bag seemed far too cosy to vacate.

I'd like to tell you that the second day was as electrifying, but the truth is somewhat more mundane. The fishing high point was unsacking my fish when the daylight was sufficient and just looking at it, trying to take it all in. I was also able to verify it as a true roach, like the others Keith had taken from this lake. (For the record, mouth shape and fin alignment were perfect, there were forty-three scales along the lateral line, eleven branched rays behind the anal fin spines, with nine behind the dorsal spines.) Then the photos and, after returning the fish and watching it kick off strongly, another congratulatory beer.

We never had a bite the rest of the day. I diversified my approach to present bread flake on-the-drop under a waggler, and then on the twelve-foot deep ledge using the lift method with a sliding float, but to no avail.

We were graced by the traditional 'four seasons in one day' Northern Irish weather. It felt more like five seasons to me, with an additional

effect of a largely invertebrate-based diet when this is the predominant food source, the pigments of the small animals accumulating in the skin and fins of the fish. This chimaera quality that fish possess, responding to diet, light conditions and level of stress, is why I almost never use colour as a diagnostic feature in fish identification.

The enormity of roach this big is just hard to take in, even good-quality photos doing no justice to their silver-scaled magnificence. To give you some idea, the dorsal fin of a fish of this outstanding size is the same shape and size as four of my fingers held together. For those more familiar with roach of a few ounces, or even true specimens of over two pounds that are nevertheless over a pound-and-a-half lighter than these gentle giants, the brain struggles to take it in. One can feel one's mental wiring change just looking at them in the flesh!

We released the staggering brace of fish, watching them kick off strongly. More beer then, and also a cup of tea to steady our nerves and warm our weary, chilled bodies. And then we resumed our efforts to catch more on this tempestuous yet surprising fourth day.

Between weather fronts, I persisted with float-fish bread reverse-trotted on the shelf, while my feeder-fished maggots also worked their magic. However, neither was appreciated by the fish.

After some hot food at nightfall, we retired to the bedchairs anticipating a dramatic fourth and final night's sport. However, a bitingly cold wind blasted in over the hills again, icy fingers mocking the ever-flapping summer-weight tent and probing every crack in the sleeping bag.

I rose with the lark to greet the fifth and last morning. Fortunately, the lark wasn't up early, hiding like me from the biting wind until about half-past eight! Much as I'd like to write about a grand finale, our session instead whimpered to a halt with neither a knock nor rolling fish to greet us.

So, how do you sum up such a session?

I'd managed just one bite in close to 230 rod-hours. Looked at another way, Keith and I had taken three roach for 11 lb! Keith had also brought to eight his tally of roach substantially bigger than the formal Irish best, though neither of us would be claiming any record.

Hard fishing, by any standards, particularly when you consider the extreme Northern Irish weather we had to endure. Bear in mind also Keith's six successive blanks prior to this trip, and you begin to appreciate the huge commitment that brought him the British record. And that is, of course, before we consider the years of diligent location that delivered his 'overnight success'.

I had anticipated far less in calculating this trip. After all, to expect a 3 lb+ roach would be to plan for insanity. My aim had been to meet up with Keith, and simply hang out with him for the craic by his special lake. Keith had another aim in mind, which he'd kept to himself: he wanted to help me break my personal best roach. No pressure there then! Happily, we both met our aspirations.

And this really sums up the Northern Irish specimen angling experience. Hard, very hard, and all of it pioneer fishing within huge swathes of unexplored potential. But boy, what potential! Especially when you consider that, in this harsher northerly climate, none of these fish yet carried an ounce of spawn and, like Keith's 4 lb 4 oz fish last year, could be 18% heavier later in the season. To save you the maths, that's a boggling 4 lb 11½oz.

That was not the last time that Keith and I fished together. We've fished for tench in England and I have been back to Keith's lake to hunt those massive roach. My best fish in later years was a fabulous roach of 2 lb 13 oz, and Keith's tally of 3 lb+ roach increased but trickled to a halt.

Over much talking and much beer, our conclusion is that the lake must have suffered a catastrophic pollution at some point in the past, just a few roach surviving and growing on without competition. At their peak, Keith happened upon them with the awareness of what he was seeing and the skills and application to maximise his chances of landing them. Also the generosity to share this closely-guarded secret with me, for which I am forever grateful.

The record roach lake may now be a memory, as smaller fish are more plentiful and the bigger ones are no longer to be seen topping. But somewhere out in that wide expanse of Northern Irish water, and almost certainly in other expanses of water where they swim unsuspected, roach of outrageous sizes may still be finning the dark depths.

TROTTING ON

~

ONE LAST CAST FROM TWO

FELLOW ENTHUSIASTS

Centrepin, big trotting float and a 2 lb 6 oz roach from the Bristol Avon in December 2005... magic!

Trotting On

I'VE BEEN LUCKY with big roach and other specimen fishes over the years. Persistent too, or maybe just bloody-minded, but I've always tried to use my scientific insights into the fish that interest me and to apply this in a flexible, learning approach to pursuing specimen roach by design. I've done okay too, with some truly big fish. However, as the record books mainly show (with a couple of notable exceptions), any fool can fluke a big fish. What means far more to me than absolute size is to catch specimens on a consistent basis, and from more than one type of water or season. This is what excites and challenges me constantly to adapt.

I have also had a lot of fun, though perhaps as much frustration, in achieving this in over fifty years of fishing, forty of them as a consistently successful specimen angler. Roach have been my muse for the large bulk of this time. I've enjoyed taking them from mighty salmon rivers and small lowland streams, canals and overgrown brooks, lakes and gravel pits, estuaries and seemingly insignificant ponds. To work out your approach to (and to catch) a big roach in unpromising circumstances – whether on a frost-gripped day under an ice shelf, in clear water beneath a blazing summer sun, or from a pool so tiny that others pass it by – can be a bigger thrill than to bank a much bigger fish in ideal conditions from a water of known form. For this reason, I've not touched upon static, self-hooking methods in big pits known to kick out big roach on a reliable basis. Others may find fulfilment there, and indeed this approach has its own trials and rewards, but I am perhaps rather too 'old school' in my love of wild places, wildlife and the challenges of finding and presenting suitable baits to wild fish.

To be a 'one trick pony' may yield results sometimes, perhaps even replicated when the same water conditions return. That may be enough for some people, and I have no difficulty with that. For others, it may become something of a trap if they stick with what has worked for them sometimes, fearful that a different approach may perhaps cause them to miss a lucky opportunity with their tested method. It's a bit like the footballer who repeats the same banal ritual before each match to bring them luck, though knowing objectively that it won't. But I'm sure all of us anglers also fall into this trap in one way or another from time to time, such as when we pull out a favourite float or bait or go to a familiar swim rather than thinking first. My own personal madness is that I've got to wear a hat to feel confident, though I know for sure that if my headgear impresses a fish then that means it has seen me and I have probably therefore just spooked it!

So my approach is maverick, non-linear, but with its own internal logic, founded on thinking first about the fish and then how best to present an acceptable bait to them. Often, I find, the predictable is merely a mask for habit. My maverick, fish-first approach has served me very well in angling for other members of the carp family across the world, including for example casting for mahseer using mangoes with dramatic success in Indian rivers, free-lining bread or worms for yellowfish in South African rivers, and so forth. And, of course, it has proven somewhat successful in my approach to specimen roach.

My roaching life to date has been a constantly surprising journey of learning and adaptation throughout the seasons of the year. I have tried to share some of this richness in the preceding pages, but it is a frustration to be unable to mention even more of the special sights, sounds, smells and experiences along the way. Also to fail to find space to write more about the diverse folks I have met and with whom I have shared these experiences, some, as in any walks of life manipulative and self-obsessed but, far, far more consistently, fascinating folk with their own enthralling tales and methods, commitments, secrets and characters.

I've been lucky enough to land, at the time I write, well over 900 roach of two pounds or more, including eleven of three pounds or greater, and from a wide range of different waters. I'm not sure why I have been this lucky, or indeed even why I'm so obsessed with the species, but I do seem to be luckier that most at least in this respect. Perhaps I was just born smeared with some weird kind of 'roach glue'!

This level of lifetime success may be unparalleled but, more importantly, it has been a fun-filled journey of discovery and innovation, some of the lessons and rich experiences of which I am only too happy to share.

Yup, catching big fish is and should be fun. If it isn't, go and do something else that is. Or, more innovatively, try fishing in a different, more rewarding way. There are a few tips scattered throughout the preceding pages to help you experiment with this.

Good luck!

Roach, including some absolute whoppers, spawning on Avon Roach Project spawning boards

The fruits of much hard labour: a net full of fit young roach are transferred from rearing tanks ready to be grown on in riverside ponds

One Last Cast
from Two Fellow Enthusiasts

THE ROACH HAS an almost unrivalled reverence in angling, and the sight of a big roach is welcome in just about any swim by anglers throughout the country, be they after chub, barbel, dace, grayling or tench.

In this modern age of peptide leakage rates and amino acid profiles, boilies, back leads and bolt rigs, this book by a fellow 'roach nut' is a breath of fresh air and a delightful journey through the life sentence that is roach fanaticism. It tells a very familiar story to those similarly afflicted.

The uncontaminated purity and simple approach that has existed for generations in roach fishing is very infectious, like stepping off the bandwagon; this is captured perfectly in this book.

The wonderfully enigmatic roach has enriched the lives of so many down the generations, but sadly is now in perilous decline in some parts of the country. So the likes of those seen here in this book are far rarer than most folk could imagine. In fact, a three pound roach is probably one of the rarest creatures in Britain today. It is this decline that has diverted our focus from the pursuit of them to the Avon Roach Project and the unbridled obsession of helping the reinstatement of a self-sustaining population in the famous and iconic Hampshire Avon, a river than once abounded and sparkled with them.

We are doing this by collecting spawn from some of the remaining population of roach on our own artificial spawning boards, which we have designed and created using short lengths of untreated scaffold boards with tresses of netting (ironically, that which is used to make keepnets) stapled to them, replicating *Fontinalis* (willow moss) which is one of the preferred natural substrates upon which roach like to spawn. Once the roach have spawned, we remove some of the boards and hatch the fish in fry tanks in Trevor's back garden, now lovingly known as Project HQ, and raise them to just short of one year old. They are then removed and relocated to a number of stews and ponds

Welcome to your new home: the young roach are released to grown on in
relative safety in rearing ponds

we have been given by generous supporters, where they remain for a
further two years. The empty tanks are then ready to do it all again.

At between three and four years of age, and on the brink of sexual
maturity, the roach are released back into the Avon, where they will
hopefully be able to increase their own numbers naturally. The release
locations are chosen very carefully, and so far have been in places
that once held good populations of roach or have undergone habitat
restoration initiatives (some in partnership and co-funded by us). And
of course we make sure to put plenty back in the locations from which
we collected spawn, making sure we give more than we take, and
ensuring we bolster the residual population from which we borrow.

Doing it this way, we retain the genetic integrity of the true Avon
Roach. We simply raise adults from the eggs of these fish in a protected
environment, unaffected by predation, starvation, flood or drought.

In nature, it is all about numbers; be it the wildebeest in Africa, our
own barn owls and honey bees, and indeed the roach in our rivers and
streams, ponds and lakes.

We see it that all we are doing is sticking our toe in the ecological
plug-hole for a while to allow the tub to fill a little to a more healthy
and self-sustainable level.

And this is what it is all about: Trevor Harrop releases a net brimming with fit and healthy 3-4 year-old roach back into the Hampshire Avon

And, as we always say, 'We must try to save them, as without roach the Avon has lost some of its soul'.

The project has grown way beyond what we both had in mind at the start. It has the full backing and support of the Environment Agency and many of the land owners up and down the valley, as well as many other river organisations, trusts and fishing clubs who are looking to our project for help and inspiration. It is independently funded through generous donations and our annual fundraising event, drug dealing and prostitution.

Our efforts and exploits can be seen and followed at www. avonroachproject.co.uk

However, whether actually doing it or simply reading a good book about it, the roach fishing itch still requires a good scratch now and then, and this book does just that.

Trevor Harrop and Budgie Price